The Bush Theat

HOW LOVE IS SPELT

By Chloë Moss
29 September - 23 October 2004

Cast

(In order of appearance)

Peta	**Kay Lyon**
Joe	**Joe Armstrong**
Steven	**Roger Evans**
Chantelle	**Petra Letang**
Marion	**Joanne Pearce**
Colin	**Colin Tierney**

Director	**Julie Anne Robinson**
Designer	**Nathalie Gibbs**
Lighting Design	**Johanna Town**
Sound Design	**Mike Walker**
Deputy Stage Manager	**Saira Anna Baker**
Assistant Stage Manager	**Justine Turton**

Press Representation   **Alexandra Gammie**
020 7833 2627

Graphic Design   **Emma Cooke at Stem Design**

With special thanks to Tom Whitemore, executor of the Sheila Lemon Bursary.

How Love Is Spelt received its world premiere at The Bush Theatre on 1st October 2004.

At The Bush Theatre

Artistic Director	**Mike Bradwell**
Executive Producer	**Fiona Clark**
General Manager	**Brenda Newman**
Literary Manager	**Nicola Wilson**
Marketing Manager	**Gillian Jones**
Production Manager	**Pam Vision**
Technical Manager	**Matt Kirby**
Resident Stage Manager	**Ros Terry**
Literary Assistant	**Holly Hughes**
Assistant General Manager	**Nic Wass**
Box Office Supervisor	**Dominique Gerrard**
Box Office Assistants	**Rowan Bangs**
	Amanda Wright
Front of House Duty	**Adrian Christopher**
Managers	**Sarah Hunter**
	Lois Tucker
	Catherine Nix-Collins
	Sarah O'Neill
Associate Artists	**Tanya Burns**
	Es Devlin
Sheila Lemon Writer in Residence	**Jennifer Farmer**

The Bush Theatre continues to develop its Writers Development Programme with the generous support of the Peggy Ramsay Foundation Award 2002.

The Bush Theatre
Shepherds Bush Green
London W12 8QD

The Alternative Theatre Company Ltd. (The Bush Theatre) is a
Registered Charity number: 270080.
Co. registration number 1221968. VAT no. 228 3168 73.

Joe Armstrong Joe

Theatre credits include *Protection* (Soho Theatre).

Television credits include *Midsomer Murders* (Bentley Productions), *Foyle's War* (Greenlit Productions), *Blackpool* (BBC), *Waking The Dead* (BBC), *Passer By* (BBC), *Between The Sheets* (Rollem Productions) and *The Bill* (Thames TV).

Roger Evans Steven

Theatre credits include *Art And Guff* (Soho Theatre/Sgript Cymru), *Everything Must Go* (Sherman Theatre), *Gas Station Angel* (Royal Court/Tour), *Scum And Civility*, *The Man Who Never Yet Saw Woman's Nakednesss* (Royal Court/International Festivals), *Crash* (Tour).

Television credits include *Murphy's Law* (Tiger Aspect), *Absolute Power* (BBC), *Nuts & Bolts* (HTV/Carlton), *Casualty* (BBC), *The Bench/The Bench II* (BBC), *Bradford In My Dreams* (BBC), *Sleeping With The TV On* (HTV Wales), *A Mind To Kill* (Fiction Factory), *Rhinoceros* (Granada), *Syth* (S4C), *Crime Traveller* (Carnival Films), *The Bill* (Thames TV) and *Wonderful You* (Hartswood Film).

Radio credits include *Station Road* and *The Member of Penbanog* (BBC Wales).

Film Credits include *All or Nothing* (Thin Man Films), *Human Traffic* (Fruit Salad Films) and *Suckerfish* (BBC Wales).

Petra Letang Chantelle

Theatre credits include *Badnuff* (Soho Theatre), *Fallout* (Royal Court), *Beautiful Thing* (Nottingham Playhouse/Tour), *Generations Of The Dead* (Young Vic), *Breath Room* (Royal Court) and *Rough Road To Survival* (Royal Court).

Television credits include *Wondrous Oblivion* (APT Film Ltd), *Babyfather* (BBC) and *Family Affairs* (Channel 5).

Radio credits include *Tell Tale* (BBC Radio).

Kay Lyon Peta

Kay graduated this year with a BTEC in Performing Arts from Southport College.

She won Best Newcomer at the Royal Television Society Awards for her performance in the leading role of Joanna in *Pleasureland*, a feature length drama produced by Kudos and shown on Channel 4 in November 2003.

Other television credits include *North and South* (BBC).

Joanne Pearce Marion

Previous Bush Theatre credits: *A Place At The Table*, *Shang-A-Lang*, *Unsuitable For Adults* (for which she won Fringe Best Actress Time Out Award) and *Love Field*. Other theatre credits include *A Woman Of No Importance* (Theatre Royal, Haymarket), *Life After George* (Duchess), *Ancient Lights* (Hampstead Theatre), *Arcadia* (Haymarket Theatre), *Therese Raquin* (Chichester Festival Theatre), *Pain Of Youth* (Gate Theatre), *Serious Money* (Wyndhams and New York) and *The Entertainer* (Shaftesbury Theatre).

Royal Shakespeare Company credits include *The Lion, The Witch and The Wardrobe*, *Little Eyolf*, *Cymbeline*, *Hamlet*, *Henry IV*, *The Alchemist*, *The Theban Plays*, *The Bybbuk*, *Twelfth Night*, *The Plantagents*, *The Plain Dealer* and *The Master Builder*.

Television credits include *Messiah 3* (BBC), *Murphy's Law* (Tiger Aspect), *The Jury* (Granada), *Silent Witness* (BBC), *Shakespeare Workshop* (BBC), *Lovejoy* (BBC), *For The Greater God* (BBC), *Way Upstream*, *The Two Gentlemen of Verona*, *The Comedy of Errors* and *Jumping The Queue* (BBC).

Film credits include *Morons From Outer Space*, *Whoops Apocalypse* and *Murder East, Murder West*.

Colin Tierney Colin

Theatre credits include *The Seagull*, *Cold Meat Party* (Royal Exchange Theatre, Manchester), *Exiles* (The Young Vic), *Duchess of Malfi* (RSC), *Hamlet* (Bristol Old Vic), *Death of Cool* (Hampstead Theatre), *Guiding Star* (National Theatre), *Othello* (National & World Tour), *Ivanov* (Almeida), *The Machine Wreckers* (National Theatre), *Henry VI* (RSC Tour), *The Life of Galileo* (Almeida), *Look Back in Anger* (Plymouth), *No Remission* (Tour), and *Sienna Red* (Peter Hall Co.).

Television credits include *Silent Witness* (BBC), *The Walk* (Granada TV), *Island at War* (Granada TV), *The Bill* (Thames Television), *Serious and Organised* (Company Pictures), *Foyle's War* (Greenlit/ITV), *The Vice* (Carlton), *Holby City* (BBC), *Mersey Beat* (ITV), *Tough Love* (Granada), *Midsomer Murders* (Bentley Productions), *Casualty* (BBC), *Soldier Soldier* (Central), *Between The Lines* (BBC), *Mandy and Sandy* (LWT), *Cracker* (Granada TV), *An Unsuitable Job For A Woman* (Ecosse/HTV) and *McCallum* (STV).

Radio credits include *Anthony and Cleopatra*, *The Last Dare* and *Macbeth*.

Film credits include *Bye, Bye Baby* (Harbour Films).

Chloë Moss Writer

Chloë's first play *Day in Dull Armour* was produced by The Royal Court Theatre, for which she won the Young Writers Festival, 2002. Chloë was the Sheila Lemon Writer in Residence at The Bush Theatre (2003/4) and is currently Writer in Residence at Paines Plough. She is under commission by Manchester Royal Exchange, The Royal Court Theatre, and The Liverpool Everyman.

Julie Anne Robinson Director

Julie Anne Robinson began by directing Shakespeare for her own company, and was a staff director at the RSC for two years. She moved into new writing and combined working at various London theatres (incl. The Royal Court, Hampstead and the National) with lots of work overseas (incl. Australia, Slovenia, Italy, Israel-West Bank). Her favourite theatre is The Bush where she has been lucky enough to direct *Yard* by Kate O' Reilly and *A Place at The Table* by Simon Block. More recently she has also worked in television, including a very enjoyable stint at Channel 4 in script development. As a director in TV her work includes *No Angels, Cutting It, Blackpool*.

Nathalie Gibbs Designer

Nathalie is a design director specialising in creating sensory brand experiences. During her time in theatre she designed for The Almeida, The Royal National Theatre, The Royal Court and The Bush.

Her work has been rewarded through a D&AD nomination, a Design Week award and FX award for an interactive installation for Orange. Over the past year she has been working on a series of experiential installations for Mercedes Benz which will be opening in 2006. Her work can also be seen in the BBC Broadcast reception and the Tate Modern in November.

Johanna Town Lighting Designer

Johanna has been Head of Lighting at the Royal Court since 1990 where recent lighting designs include *Food Chain*, *Under the Whaleback*, *Terrorism*, *Plasticine* and *Where Do We Live*.

Her freelance lighting designs include *A Permanent Way*, *She Stoops to Conquer*, *A Laughing Matter* (Out Of Joint/RNT), *Shopping & Fucking* (Out of Joint & West End), *The Steward of Christendom* (Out of Joint & Broadway), *I.D.* (Almeida), *Six Degrees of Separation*, *Ghosts* (Royal Exchange), *The Dumb Waiter* (Oxford Playhouse), *Brassed Off* (Liverpool Playhouse, Birmingham Rep), *Badnuff*, *Mr Nobody* (Soho Theatre); *Feelgood*, *Little Malcolm & His Struggle Against the Eunuchs* (both Hampstead & West End), *Rose* (RNT/Broadway), *Via Dolorosa*, *Top Girls* (West End), *Arabian Nights*, *Our Lady of Sligo* (both New York). She also lit *Guantanemo Bay* for the Tricycle Theatre in the West End and currently on Broadway.

Mike Walker Sound Designer

Mike first worked at the Grand Theatre, Wolverhampton before training at The Guildhall School of Music and Drama in London. He started working in sound at The Coliseum Theatre, Oldham.

Sound designs include *Carousel* (National Theatre, Shaftesbury Theatre and Tokyo), *Oliver!* (London Palladium), *The Graduate* (London and Australia), *The Full Monty* (London and UK Tour), *Jus' Like That* (Garrick Theatre and UK Tour) and *Jerry Springer - The Opera* (Edinburgh and London), which won the 2004 Olivier Award for Best Sound Design, *Songs My Mother Taught Me* with Lorna Luft (Savoy Theatre) and *Bat Boy - The Musical* (West Yorkshire Playhouse and Shaftesbury Theatre).

He was invited to Singapore in 1994 to design *Into The Woods* and has designed over twenty productions there since, including *Little Shop of Horrors*, *Sing To The Dawn*, *Hamlet*, *Art*, *They're Playing Our Song* (Singapore and Manila), *Chang & Eng* (Singapore, Bangkok and Kuala Lumpur) and *Forbidden City* which formed part of the opening festival of the *Esplanade - Theatres on The Bay*.

On a consultancy basis he has worked for the National Theatre; Theatre Royal, Stratford East; Albany Theatre, Deptford; Singapore Repertory Theatre and the Royal Academy of Music.

The Bush Theatre

The Bush Theatre opened in April 1972 in the upstairs dining room of The Bush Hotel, Shepherds Bush Green. The room had previously served as Lionel Blair's dance studio. Since then, The Bush has become the country's leading new writing venue with over 350 productions, premiering the finest new writing talent.

"One of the most vibrant theatres in Britain, and a consistent hotbed of new writing talent."
Midweek magazine

Playwrights whose works have been performed here at The Bush include:

Stephen Poliakoff, Robert Holman, Tina Brown, Snoo Wilson, John Byrne, Ron Hutchinson, Terry Johnson, Beth Henley, Kevin Elyot, Doug Lucie, Dusty Hughes, Sharman Macdonald, Billy Roche, Tony Kushner, Catherine Johnson, Philip Ridley, Richard Cameron, Jonathan Harvey, Richard Zajdlic, Naomi Wallace, David Eldridge, Conor McPherson, Joe Penhall, Helen Blakeman, Lucy Gannon, Mark O'Rowe and Charlotte Jones.

The theatre has also attracted major acting and directing talents including Bob Hoskins, Alan Rickman, Antony Sher, Stephen Rea, Frances Barber, Lindsay Duncan, Brian Cox, Kate Beckinsale, Patricia Hodge, Simon Callow, Alison Steadman, Jim Broadbent, Tim Roth, Jane Horrocks, Gwen Taylor, Mike Leigh, Mike Figgis, Mike Newell and Richard Wilson.

Victoria Wood and Julie Walters first worked together at The Bush, and Victoria wrote her first sketch on an old typewriter she found backstage.

In over 30 years, The Bush has won over one hundred awards and recently received The Peggy Ramsay Foundation Project Award 2002. Bush plays, including most recently *The Glee Club*, have transferred to the West End. Off-Broadway transfers include *Howie the Rookie* and *Resident Alien*. Film adaptations include *Beautiful Thing* and *Disco Pigs*. Bush productions have toured throughout Britain, Europe and North America, most recently *Stitching*. In March 2004 *Adrenalin... Heart* represented the UK in the Tokyo International Arts Festival. *The Glee Club* by Richard Cameron is currently touring the UK - more details can be found at our website (www.bushtheatre.co.uk).

Every year we receive over fifteen hundred scripts through the post, and we read them all. According to The Sunday Times:

"What happens at The Bush today is at the very heart of tomorrow's theatre"

That's why we read all the scripts we receive and will continue to do so.

Mike Bradwell   **Fiona Clark**
Artistic Director   **Executive Producer**

Be There At The Beginning

The Bush Theatre is a writer's theatre – dedicated to commissioning, developing and producing exclusively new plays. Up to seven writers each year are commissioned and we offer a bespoke programme of workshops and one-to-one dramaturgy to develop their plays. Our international reputation of over thirty years is built on consistently producing the very best work to the very highest standard.

With your help this work can continue to flourish.

The Bush Theatre's Patron Scheme delivers an exciting range of opportunities for individual and corporate giving, offering a closer relationship with the theatre and a wide range of benefits from ticket offers to special events. Above all, it is an ideal way to acknowledge your support for one of the world's greatest new writing theatres.

To join, please pick up an information pack from the foyer, call 020 7602 3703 or email info@bushtheatre.co.uk

We would like to thank our current members and invite you to join them!

Rookies
Anonymous
Anonymous
David Brooks
Sian Hansen
Lucy Heller
Mr G Hopkinson
Ray Miles
Malcolm & Liliane Ogden
Clare Rich & Robert Marshall
Martin Shenfield
Loveday Weymouth

Beautiful Things
Alan Brodie
Clive Butler
Clyde Cooper
Patrick and Anne Foster
Vivien Goodwin
Sheila Hancock
David Hare
William Keeling
Adam Kenwright
Laurie Marsh
John Reynolds
Mr and Mrs George Robinson
Tracey Scoffield
Barry Serjent
Brian D Smith

Glee Club
Anonymous
The Hon Mrs Giancarla Alen-Buckley
Jim Broadbent
Stephen Lovegrove and Kate Brooke
Nick Marston
Shirley Robson

Lone Star
Silver Star

Bronze Corporate Membership
Act Productions Ltd

Silver Corporate Membership
The Agency

Platinum Corporate Membership
Anonymous

HOW LOVE IS SPELT

Chloë Moss

For

Patricia, Ken and Nick Moss

Nick B – At the very beginning . . .

Love to my friends and a big thank you
to the following, for their help with *How Love Is Spelt*

All at The Bush, Tom Whitemore for the Sheila Lemon
Bursary, Mel Kenyon, Simon Stephens, Colette Kane,
John Tiffany, Michelle Morgan, The Peggy Ramsay
Foundation, Chris McGill at milktwosugars,
Mark Monero, Phillip Bosworth, Katherine Parkinson,
Jem Wall and Rebecca Palmer

Characters

PETA, *twenty*

JOE, *thirty-two*

STEVEN, *thirty*

CHANTELLE, *twenty-two*

MARION, *forty-nine*

COLIN, *forty-two*

Scene One

PETA*'s bedsit. Small and sparse. A door leads to the bathroom. An arch leads through to a tiny kitchen area. In the middle of the living area there is a sofa bed which is never used as a sofa. Along one wall is a small tatty armchair and a chest of drawers with a TV on and a large black-and-white photo of a man in his thirties.*

JOE *is lying sprawled out on the bed, hands behind his head. After a few moments he gets up and starts looking about the room. He picks the photo up and studies it, then opens the top drawer of the chest slowly so as not to make any noise. He stares into the drawer for a few seconds then carefully slides it shut. After a quick nose through the kitchen he resumes his place on the bed.*

JOE. You alright in there?

> *Pause. No reply.*

> Petra . . . You OK in there, darlin'?

> *No reply.*

> Petra, you OK?

> *No reply.*

> You want anything, sweetheart?

> *A few more moments then the door opens and* PETA *appears, dressed in an oversize T-shirt;* JOE*'s. She walks over to the armchair and sits down on it, pulling her chest up to her knees.*

> You alright?

PETA. Yeah. Thanks.

JOE. Thought you'd legged it . . . shot out the bathroom window or something.

PETA. I live here.

JOE. Yeah.

PETA. I washed your shirt. Sorry about that.

JOE. S'alright . . . happens to the best of us.

PETA. Sorry.

JOE. Don't . . . don't you worry about it. (*Beat.*) Didn't think you were that gone, though, to tell the truth. Didn't seem that . . . pissed.

PETA. No. I can't take –

JOE. You're little. Petite . . . don't take much on a little frame. I could drink a fucking . . . brewery and make it home upright. Fuckin' . . . beer monster.

Pause.

PETA. You want anything? Cup of tea? toast?

JOE. You got anything to go on it?

PETA. On what?

JOE. Toast . . . jam or anything . . . Marmite.

PETA. No. Sorry.

JOE. Just a cuppa tea'd be nice then, sweetheart.

She gets up and goes into the kitchen.

I don't like plain toast . . . like a bit of flavour. Don't really taste of much . . . bread, does it? On its own.

Pause.

S'nice this place, innit? Little but nice.

PETA. S'alright.

JOE. They sting you for rent?

PETA. Not too bad.

JOE. What's 'not too bad' . . . if you don't mind me being nosey. Just wondering cos, you know, nice little place like this. Zone what . . . Two, is it?

PETA. Yeah –

JOE. Thought, you know. Do you get stung?

PETA. It's an old student place. Sixty-five quid a week.

JOE. Sixty-five quid a week?

PETA. Yeah.

JOE. Yeah? Bloody hell, you landed on your feet there, didn't yer?

Pause.

PETA. There's no teabags.

JOE. Coffee?

Pause.

PETA. No. Sorry, just milk . . . or water.

JOE. Is it alright?

PETA. Is what?

JOE. The milk. I got nothing against milk but if it's off, like a day or so out . . . makes me fucking heave.

PETA. No, it's alright. I got it yesterday.

JOE. Full-fat or semi-skimmed? . . . Or skimmed? I hate fucking . . . hate skimmed milk . . . s'like white water. I don't see the point in skimmed milk.

PETA. It's just normal. Full fat.

JOE. Go on then, yeah. I'll have a glass of milk. I haven't had milk since I was . . .

PETA. I love milk.

Pause.

JOE. I had a good time last night, Petra. Enjoyed meself.

No reply.

At that place, yer know, and then . . . back here. Back at yours. Did you?

No reply.

Petra?

She enters with the tea, hands it to him and sits back down in the armchair.

PETA. It's Peta.

JOE. Sorry?

PETA. It's Peta, not Petra . . . you keep saying Petra and it's Peta.

JOE. Peta? Fuckin' hell, sorry darlin' . . . why didn't you say?

PETA. I did.

JOE. Last night. Why didn't you say something last night?

PETA. I did.

JOE. Fuckin' . . . Sorry babe. I must 'ave been well gone . . . I didn't think I was but I fuckin' must 'ave been, eh? I'm sorry about that, sweetheart. That's like fuckin' . . . disrespectful . . . that is. Getting a woman's name wrong. Peta. (*Pause.*) Peta. Ain't that a bloke's name though?

PETA. If you're a bloke.

JOE. Yeah 'course. Sorry, I didn't mean –

PETA. It's spelt with an 'a' instead of 'e-r'. P-e-t-a.

JOE. Right . . . pretty that. Peta. Pretty name. Pretty girl . . . Pretty Peta.

Long pause.

I was just saying . . . Peta . . . I enjoyed meself last night.

PETA. Right.

JOE. Did you?

PETA. It was alright. I didn't like that place much –

JOE. No . . . yeah, I know what you mean, it's a fuckin' dive that place . . . dunno why I keep going back . . . but afterwards, back here –

PETA. Like a cattle market. I don't like it when it's like that somewhere.

JOE. I know what you mean –

PETA. Don't know where some people get off –

JOE. But I enjoyed meself with you . . . s'all I'm saying. Back here rather than . . . in there. In the place.

PETA. Right.

JOE. Cheap ale though.

PETA. What?

JOE. In the . . . in that place . . . ale's cheap. I'm just thinking, 'Why do I keep going back?' and I just thought then. Cheap ale. You can get tanked up and fuck off somewhere else. Somewhere better. Or you get tanked up and just fucking stay cos you can't be arsed going anywhere else . . . which is what I usually do. When I go there. Which isn't all the time. I don't go every fucking week . . . just sometimes. I go sometimes (*Beat.*) Glad I went last night.

Pause. JOE *starts to drum his leg self-consciously and whistle through his teeth.* PETA *stares ahead.*

You ain't got a fella, have you?

PETA. No.

JOE. Right . . . no, sorry, it's just you seem a bit . . . seems like you're a bit edgy. On edge.

PETA. No . . . I'm just a bit –

JOE. Sure . . . yeah, sorry . . . take no notice, I'm just being . . . it wasn't nothing really. You just seemed a bit –

PETA. On edge.

JOE. A bit.

PETA. No. I'm fine –

JOE. If you want me to go –

PETA. You're fine –

JOE. Just say, you know . . . don't feel –

PETA. You're fine.

JOE. I don't wanna outstay me welcome, s'all.

Pause.

PETA. It's fine.

JOE (*gesturing to photo on top of TV*). That your old man?

PETA. Yeah.

JOE. I knew that.

PETA. Did you?

JOE. Yeah. Has he . . . Is he dead?

Pause.

PETA. Yeah.

JOE. Fuck . . . is he?

PETA. Yeah. Why'd you say it?

JOE. I didn't think. I just knew. Instinct. S'mad that, isn't it? (*Beat.*) I dunno . . . You can sort of tell. Head and shoulders, black-and-white . . . top of the telly. Makes you think that they're dead. Dunno quite why. It's like . . . that size as well. Big . . . like . . . a tribute. To someone who's dead. (*Beat.*) Jesus . . . get in there, Joe, stick your fuckin' boot in. Fuckin' 'ell . . . I do that when I get –

PETA. S'alright –

JOE. – Nervous . . . well, not nervous but . . . fucking . . . when I start down a road that I really shouldn't be going down. I don't know you. I shouldn't be talking about . . . your dad and if he's dead or –

PETA. I don't mind. It was a long time . . . ages ago.

JOE. Right. Still. He . . . go . . . pass on . . . when you were little?

She nods.

Accident?

PETA. Cancer.

JOE. Yeah . . . thought so, always fuckin' that, ain't it? Or the heart. One of the two. How old were you?

PETA. Seven.

JOE. Fuckin' . . . sad. You close to him?

PETA. Yeah . . . only remember bits and bobs now though. Little flickers.

JOE. I hardly remember my old man. Good thing by all accounts, he was a bit of a bad lot, you know the sort. Dunno why he bothered havin' us . . . well, he didn't really, did he? Did the neccessary which don't take long and then came back every now an' then when he felt like reminding himself that he'd done something half-decent in his life. Buffer himself up, y'know? He was a cunt an' half.

PETA. He was there. My dad.

JOE. Was he?

PETA. Yes. He was there. Properly.

JOE. You're lucky . . . well, you know what I mean. At least you got some nice memories. They go a long way, nice memories.

PETA. I've got a few. I remember some bits . . . good ones . . . not loads, but they're good.

JOE. They go a long way.

PETA. I did shows for him, in the front room. Dancing.

JOE. Dancing. Right.

PETA. On a Saturday. After *Grandstand*. Have you got kids?

Pause.

JOE. No . . . well, yeah I have, it's just – I've got a little girl.

PETA. Have you?

JOE. Yeah.

PETA. How old is she?

JOE (*thinks*). Nine. She'll be nine now . . . just about. Nine in . . . May. Actually. I don't see her. She's called Hayley. I don't see her, not since she was a baby. I didn't leave her.

PETA. What happened?

JOE. Her mother. Brenda. She was only young – I ain't blaming her . . . she was . . . a kid herself really. We went out . . . only a few times. I never asked her properly, asked her out, properly, you know. Don't know why now. I wanted – She was a lovely looking girl. Lived up an estate on the Lee Bridge Road . . . family rough as arseholes but she had other stuff in her head, you know. Bright as a button. Beautiful girl. I thought it was gonna work out alright at first. (*Pause.*) Her dad . . . the bloke she – her mum, Brenda, married, he's in the army. Cyprus. Nice place for a kid to be, that, isn't it? Like being on holiday all the time. Speaking Spanish. (*Beat.*) I don't . . . haven't been out there. It's confusing, you know. For her. Ain't fair, that.

PETA. You're her dad.

JOE. No.

PETA. Don't you ever just want to get on a plane and see her . . . see what she looks like?

JOE. I know what she looks like . . . in me head. Spitting image of me. But pretty. I got a picture. She's just a baby in it but you can't half tell . . . see what she'd be like now. I imagine that a lot. It seems real after a bit . . . I'd get a shock if she was different . . . from in me head. Don't know how I'd . . . yer know.

Pause.

S'nice in here. Sixty-five quid. S'good that.

PETA. Don't you miss her?

JOE. Can't miss something you never had. I love her though. I do love her. Love the idea of her. The thought of her. Nice memories again, you see . . . get you a long way. She looked like . . . I don't know, I can't explain it. I ain't good at all that . . . but she . . . it was like someone coming and ripping your heart out yer chest. It was like . . . five minutes. Like a little dream. They moved now. I haven't got the address. Gets me a bit mad that sometimes. Gets me fuckin' . . . She might come round looking for me one day. Give me a piece of her mind. I'll have to do all that . . . explaining.

PETA. Are you cold?

JOE. No.

Pause.

PETA. Your mate'll wonder what happened to you. Won't he? Be wondering why you left. Will he have a go at yer?

JOE. Martin? Let him try. Nah . . . blokes for you, ain't it? If it's a bird, it's allowed . . . you get points. Last week I catch Martin trying a skulk out of Legends – this late place we always go Wednesdays in Streatham – cos he reckons he's tired . . . fuckin' queer. Now that ain't allowed but pulling . . . you can't get stick for that. Anyway, had to do the gentlemanly thing, didn't I? Escort you home, damsel in distress . . . on her own and all . . . not that I'm being sexist or anything, that's one thing I've learnt – don't be sexist in front of birds, they hate it.

Pause.

That was a joke.

PETA (*stares at him*). I know.

JOE. Wasn't sure whether to come over . . . you looked a bit . . . lost. Bit sad. But I thought . . . give it a whirl . . . see what happens. My rule number one is . . . you shouldn't chat to people if they don't chat back. Something terrible might just have happened or they might just be miserable cunts. Either way, they're not gonna wanna chat to you, are they?

PETA *doesn't respond.*

How come you were on your own, anyway? Not on the game, are yer?

PETA. Fuck off.

JOE. Aah, come on darlin', that was another one . . . sorry . . .
you don't wanna take no notice of me, I'm a wind-up
merchant . . . gets me in trouble most the time. I forget
meself.

PETA. I told you, anyway . . . my mate . . . met this bloke,
must have left with him. I was on the way out, sick of
looking for them . . . doing laps like some idiot.

JOE. You were sat down. I thought you'd been stood up.

PETA. No, I was just . . . hangin' on . . . finishing me drink,
about to get off.

JOE. 'Til I saw you . . . through the crowd . . . like a vision. A
vision in purple.

Pause.

Bet you get loads of that, don't yer?

PETA. What?

JOE. Blokes . . . comin' on to yer . . . giving it all that.

Silence.

Don'tcha?

PETA. No.

JOE. Give over . . . blinder like you . . . bet you 'ave them
queuing . . . eh?

PETA. Not – no.

JOE. C'mon . . . I ain't as green as I'm cabbage-lookin'. Bet
you 'ave them queuing.

PETA. I don't.

JOE. Blinder like you . . . little belter? You're being modest.
Bet you 'ave 'em . . . fucking . . . snaking around the block –

PETA. No.

JOE. All like . . . begging to take you out –

PETA. Please shut up . . . I don't, will you just –

JOE. Going on with meself there. Sorry.

PETA. S'alright.

JOE. Get carried away with meself sometimes.

PETA. S'alright.

JOE. I don't mean no . . .

PETA. I know. It's fine.

Pause.

Starts again

JOE. What you doin' perched over there, anyway? Come here.

PETA. I'm sound here, thanks.

JOE. Come on . . . I feel a bit weird in your bed. You on the chair. S'your bed. We could swop if it's cos you don't want to –

PETA. No . . . I'm alright here.

Pause.

JOE. You look a lot like your old man, don't yer? I mean, you haven't got stubble obviously . . . but you got that look . . . it's the eyes, I think. You got beautiful eyes. Tell you all sorts, don't they, eyes? (*Beat.*) Listen to me. I ain't usually like this.

PETA. Like what?

JOE. Big fuckin' . . . soppy cunt. S'a compliment though, that is . . . to you. I don't normally have . . . I can't be arsed normally. Not my thing. I got a real . . . string . . . in my step today.

PETA *smirks.*

What?

PETA. That doesn't make any sense.

JOE. Eh?

PETA. String. You don't get a string in your step. You get a spring in your step.

JOE. Oh no. Really?

PETA (*laughing*). Yeah. Spring . . . like you're bouncing.

JOE. Fuck. Yeah. 'Course. I do that all the time (*Beat.*) What's a fuckin' . . . piece of sodding string got to do with anything, eh? See, I never think. I just fuckin' . . . I'm always getting things wrong, but I never notice. People are always pulling me up. Taking the piss. I'd never notice otherwise . . . if they didn't take the piss.

PETA. It's funny.

JOE. S'fuckin' stupid. They thought I was dyslexic in school . . . for years. Got proper special treatment, the works. Turned out I was just fuckin' thick. I kept tellin' 'em but they wasn't havin' any of it. I don't care. I think it's funny. (*Pause.*) My mum used to say 'Ignorance is bliss' and lately I've just started to get me head round that. I've started noticing, right . . . this might sound a bit . . . daft, but every clever person I know is also a right miserable cunt. Like they know something that not everyone else knows. Like the fucking world's gonna end next Thursday.

PETA. It might.

JOE. I'm a glass half-full sort of person and maybe that's cos I don't know enough but if it is then . . . fuckin' . . . good. Don't teach me nothing.

Ends now - 2mins = 3mins.

Pause.

PETA. What do you do?

JOE. For work?

PETA. For anything.

JOE. I'm laid off at the moment with me back, but usually I work on the sites. I'm a hod carrier. (*Beat.*) Not yer Beckham or anything but pay ain't too bad. Lads are a laugh. Martin from last night, yeah, I met him two years ago on a job up in Newcastle . . . bonded, yer know, two blokes from Dagenham an' that. Turns out, he was three years below in the same school as me. (*Beat.*) The same school. Never met

him 'til then. In fucking Newcastle. Life is fuckin' well
spooky like that sometimes, innit?

Silence.

Makes you think, don't it?

PETA. About what?

JOE. I dunno. Fate and that.

Pause.

Yeah . . . so do that and go out with me mates, play footy
on a Sunday . . . got a little team. Get down the gym when
I can . . . if I'm not too hungover. How 'bout yourself?

PETA. What?

JOE. What d'you do?

PETA. Work?

JOE. Yeah . . . you got a job? Student . . . what? I mean, you
gotta beg my pardon a bit here, sweetheart, because you
may well have told me all this last –

PETA. I'm just . . . I want to be in advertising. I'm working
my way up . . . just from the bottom really, at an agency –
a proper one though – on the phones, taking . . . minutes . . .
notes. Just, y'know, administration for now but –

JOE. Yeah . . . no definitely, yeah. Advertising . . . bloody hell.
That's a bit . . .

PETA. What?

JOE. I dunno . . . trendy, y'know.

PETA. Not really.

JOE. You know, like . . . What d'yer call yuppies these days?

PETA. I don't know.

JOE. I ain't . . . I mean, I'm not saying anything against it . . .
that's a bloody good job.

PETA. It's not as good as it sounds . . . I'm on the bottom rung
now, but not for long hopefully. That's what you do in those

sort of places . . . work dead hard, stay late, get yourself noticed . . . eventually. Hope it isn't for long.

JOE. Not for long, I bet . . . brains, beauty. You've got it on a plate, you have, Petra.

PETA. Peta.

JOE (*hits himself on the head*). Fuck's sake . . . sorry darlin'. You can tell why I'm not a . . . an executive, can't yer? You like it then?

PETA. Yeah, it's good.

JOE. You have to do reports . . . all that sort of stuff . . . presentations?

PETA. Sometimes, yeah.

JOE. Now I admire that . . . getting up talking in front of people. I'm shit at that. Talk the hind legs off a donkey, me . . . you know, down the pub . . . talk in front of the lads, tell jokes, life and soul but . . . you get me, you put me in a . . . in a . . . formal type of set-up and I lose it. Big time. Sends me west. (*Beat.*) Good for you, darlin'. Your dad'd be well proud of that. He'll be looking . . . you know . . . looking down an' that. Well proud. I would be . . . Hayley turning up in a few years, saying she's a . . . works in advertising. Lovely that.

He finishes his milk in one gulp and sticks the cup on the floor by the side of the sofa bed.

Mind if I nip for a piss?

PETA. No.

JOE. Don't suppose I need to ask where it is really, do I? Not exactly Buckingham Palace, is it . . . I mean, you know . . . the size, I'm not –

PETA. It's just there.

He gets up, adjusting his underpants and goes into the bathroom. When the door is shut PETA jumps out of the chair and starts piling together the papers and photos that are spilling out from under the sofa. She pushes them into the top drawer of the chest and then darts back into the

*armchair, fixing herself in the same position. The door
opens and* JOE *steps out, he lies back on the bed but this
time with his head at the other end, nearer to* PETA.

JOE. I had a quick lend of your toothbrush then . . . that
alright?

PETA. Yeah.

JOE. Some people get a bit funny about that, don't they? I do
usually, but I thought . . .

PETA. S'OK.

JOE. S'nice that toothpaste . . . Herbal Colgate. Not tried that
before.

PETA. It's new.

JOE. You've got nice teeth, you have. Like teeth in a drawing.
All sort of like . . . I should have had a brace when I was a
kid . . . they're all over the shop, mine.

PETA. They're alright. They're just . . . normal.

JOE. Nah. All crooked. Like a row o' bombed houses. Would
have got battered though . . . round by ours. With a brace.
You got lovely straight ones.

PETA. Ta.

JOE. Lovely mouth.

PETA. It's too wide.

JOE. S'lovely.

PETA. Ta.

JOE. You got a proper cupid's bow. People pay good money
for that . . . get that . . . rubber stuff pumped in there –

PETA. I used to be able to get my whole fist in it when I was
little. Can't any more –

JOE. Why don't you get on here with me?

PETA. Me hand's too big. I'm alright here.

JOE. I wasn't asking how you were, I was –

PETA. I'm alright on here.

JOE. Can I take you out somewhere, Peta?

PETA. Where?

JOE. I dunno. I was gonna ask you. Where do you fancy, eh? Nice meal, one night this week? Pictures? Theatre? My mate's a ticket tout, he can get half-price tickets for *Les Miserables*. We could do that. (*Beat.*) No pressure.

Pause.

PETA. I wouldn't mind going the aquarium. The one by the big wheel.

JOE. The aquarium? Would you now? Well, I think that might be quite easy to arrange, little girl. No problem.

PETA (*unenthusiastically*). Whenever, like.

JOE. Yeah, whenever, like. Give you a little buzz . . . see when you're free –

PETA. Yeah.

JOE. Why don't you just get on here though, eh? Come on . . . don't be shy. I've gotta go soon . . . get to fuckin' work. No rest for the wicked, not even on a Saturday. Come on . . . five minutes. Bit of a cuddle. I ain't trying it on.

PETA. I just –

JOE. Come on –

PETA. Oh please . . . look, I'm really alright here. To be honest, I feel a bit – I'm not that comfy with this. I don't normally have – you know, do . . . one-night things.

JOE. Ain't one night no more, darlin'. We're next day now. This is the longest relationship I've ever had.

PETA. Yeah . . . funny, but –

JOE. I don't judge no one, darlin', you haven't done nothing wrong. This is the nineties now. Sexual liberation and all that –

PETA. It's 2004 –

JOE. All that old-fashioned bollocks about girls being ladies . . .
(*Pause.*) I'm not as green as I'm cabbage-lookin', Peta . . .
know what I'm sayin'?

PETA. Not really –

JOE. Sorry, I shouldn't start . . . philosophising. Doesn't really
get me anywhere. Look. All I'm saying is . . . I think you're
lovely, I had a lovely time last night. Weren't nothing wrong
about it . . . I don't want you feeling all weird. I hate all this
next morning stuff, s'rubbish . . . I don't do sneaking off.
Anyway, I like you. Think you're lovely.

PETA. Thanks.

JOE. Don't be thankin' me, darlin', nothing to do with me. It's
in your genes. All down to him . . . your dad . . . and your
mum, 'course. She must have been a right stunner n'all. You
take after her?

PETA. Not really.

JOE. More your dad? I can see that. Them eyes. Fuck . . .
Listen to me. Sound like a right poof. You wanna go out?
I'd like to see you again . . . take you out. You like Chinese?

PETA. Chinese what?

JOE. Food . . . what d'you think I mean? Fuckin' lanterns?

PETA. I was taking the piss.

JOE (*playfully*). Oh you was, was you?

PETA. Yeah.

JOE. You was, was you?

*He stands up and grabs her playfully, but can easily
overpower her and throws her onto the bed, diving after
her. She starts to scream but he is in his own world,
laughing and thinking she is enjoying 'the game'. He starts
to tickle her and kiss her neck and she struggles and kicks
out even more. This continues for a few more moments until
she grabs his balls really hard. He falls backwards, writhing
around in silent agony. PETA frees herself and stands
nervously at the side of the bed, watching him.*

PETA. I told yer . . . I said I was alright on the chair. I got scared.

There is no reply. He can't speak.

I thought you were – I got frightened. I told you I was alright on the chair. I didn't want –

He has begun to moan quietly.

I got a fright.

He launches himself upright, still clutching his groin.

JOE (*under his breath*). Jesus fuckin' Christ. (*Shouting.*) Are you fuckin' mad or what?

PETA. You shouldn't have –

He stands up, still in agony, trying to get himself together.

JOE. What the fuck are you playing at?

PETA. You shouldn't . . . I got a fright, I didn't know what you were doing. I don't know yer. You could be –

JOE. Could be fucking what?

Silence.

Could you get me my shirt?

PETA. I don't think it's dry yet, I could –

JOE. Could you get me my shirt?

She gets the shirt from the bathroom and hands it to him. He goes to put it on but it's too wet and he takes it off, muttering angrily under his breath. He pulls his trousers on which have been lying on the floor at the side of the bed. Shirt in hand, he stands to leave.

PETA. I could iron it for yer. Dry it off a bit –

JOE. You're a fucking loony . . . what d'you think I was doing? I'm not a fuckin' sex –

PETA. It's soakin'. I thought I was going to be sick.

JOE. Yeah well . . . I'm going now. You can chuck your guts up to your fucking heart's content.

PETA. We could still go out somewhere . . . if you wanted.

Pause. JOE *stomps around, trying to get himself together, a bit shocked and still in pain.*

JOE. You wanna watch that. Get yourself in trouble, going around –

PETA. You'll get yourself in trouble too . . . get someone's brother or dad after yer.

JOE. Are you threatening me?

PETA. I haven't got a brother and me dad's dead. I said sorry.

JOE. You wanna just . . .

PETA. Sorry. Sorry. Sorry. Sorry.

JOE. Watch what you –

PETA (*trying to be light-hearted*). You sound like my dad. Telling me off. You sound like your gonna say . . . 'young lady' or . . . something. You shouldn't – You can't be like that, not when I don't know you. You could be . . . you have to think. Sorry. I've got a T-shirt . . . I sleep in it. It's massive. You could wear that if you wanted.

JOE *stares at her for a few seconds then turns and storms out, slamming the door behind him.*

Blackout.

Scene Two

The stage is still in darkness when we hear the fumbling of a key in the lock and giggling. PETA *stumbles in and switches the light on.* STEVEN *follows meekly behind. He is late twenties/early thirties, conservatively dressed.*

PETA. Here we are.

STEVEN. This is nice.

PETA. No, it isn't. Do you want a drink?

STEVEN. Erm . . . yes please.

PETA. What d' you want?

STEVEN. Erm . . . Whatever you've got . . . lager?

PETA. Hold on. (*She roots about in the fridge.*) No . . . sorry.

STEVEN. That's OK . . . whatever you've got.

PETA. Milk.

STEVEN. Erm . . . no, it's OK, thanks.

PETA (*returning from the kitchen*). Sorry, I need to go
    shopping.

STEVEN. Don't apologise, it's fine . . . I've had enough
    already anyway.

PETA. Yeah . . . school night for you, remember.

STEVEN. I do, believe me.

PETA. Thanks.

STEVEN. What for?

PETA. Seeing me back safely. That's very –

STEVEN. Don't be silly –

PETA. Gentlemanly. That's what gentle men do. Make things
    safe. I had this ex-boyfriend come round the other week.
    I broke his . . . well, he didn't want it. For us to finish.
    He went apeshit at the time. Really mad. Really angry.
    Accusing me, you know . . . of all sorts of shit. He came
    around, anyway, the other week . . . well, I saw him out, at
    this horrible dive in Streatham. He seemed alright . . . calm,
    you know. Like the bloke I used to know . . . and that was
    comforting. But he comes back and tries it on and gets all
    aggressive . . . like just cos I'd done it with him before, you
    know . . . he can . . . anyway, I lost it and really swung for
    him. Grabbed him by the bollocks and chucked him right
    out. Not standing for any of that shit.

Pause.

STEVEN. Bloody hell.

PETA. It was fine though. I can handle myself fine. What age are they?

STEVEN. What age are what?

PETA. The kids. The ones you teach.

STEVEN. Right, yeah, erm . . . all ages really.

PETA. Secondary though? You said secondary before.

STEVEN. Yes. All the way through from Year 7 to A-levels . . . but I've got Year 9 all day tomorrow. They're the worst. We're going on a trip.

PETA. What do they do?

STEVEN. They're just . . . horrible. All hormonal and hyperactive. It's that funny age, isn't it? Sort of thirteen, fourteen.

PETA. I didn't think it was funny being thirteen.

STEVEN. Well exactly. I meant 'funny strange' as opposed to 'funny ha ha'.

PETA. Do they like you?

STEVEN. I don't know. I don't know much about them. In fact, I don't really know anything about them, to be honest. Which is a bit worrying. (*Beat.*) I can't identify with them at all. I always say to them in PSE. Er . . . which is –

PETA. Personal and Social Education –

STEVEN. Exactly. Personal and Social Education. I always say to them 'If you've got any problems at all, then . . . you know . . . please come and see me if you want to talk them through and I'll try to help in any way I can' –

PETA. I could tell that about you.

STEVEN. What's that?

PETA. You're caring. Most people aren't.

STEVEN. Well, I don't know, I mean . . . I live in absolute bloody dread that one day, one of them will come to me and try to talk to me about something . . . personal. I wouldn't have a clue.

PETA. I wouldn't worry about it. Most kids would rather boil their heads in vinegar than talk to a teacher about anything.

STEVEN. Do you think?

PETA. Oh yeah. It's like when they go, 'Is everything alright at home?' and you're like, 'Of course it fucking isn't, but as if I want to talk to you about it. You stink of mothballs.' (*Beat.*) I mean, you don't stink of mothballs but you're not like the teachers I had.

STEVEN. Is that a good thing?

PETA. Oh yeah.

STEVEN. Right. Good . . . well, let's hope you're right anyway. About the kids. (*Beat.*) I mean, I would try to help obviously . . . I wouldn't just ignore them or anything. Obviously.

Pause.

PETA. Sit down.

STEVEN. Right, yeah. Ta. (*He moves towards the chair.*)

PETA. Sit on the bed. It's a couch bed, but I don't bother with the couch bit usually. Don't have many guests.

STEVEN. Thanks.

He perches uncomfortably on the edge while PETA *clambers on and sits cross-legged in the middle.*

PETA. Where are you going?

STEVEN. Sorry?

PETA. On your trip, your day-out thing tomorrow.

STEVEN. Oh yes . . . erm . . . oh God, bloody Hampton Court.

PETA. What's wrong with that?

STEVEN. I just – it wouldn't be my first choice but it fits with the stuff I'm doing with them at the moment – Henry the Eighth and –

PETA. He lived there, didn't he?

STEVEN. Yes.

PETA. I saw that on the posters on the tubes. He was a right pig, wasn't he? Imagine that, being married to him.

STEVEN. Yes. Not much fun.

PETA. Twat. Chop your head off for eating crisps in bed.

STEVEN. Probably. So I just thought . . . you know. Combine a bit of fun with a . . . bit of education. I'm not looking forward to it all that much though, to be honest.

PETA. I used to love school trips. Especially History ones. It was me favourite subject. I used to be able to name all the Kings and Queens right through.

STEVEN. That's good. It doesn't seem to be very popular these days, History. Not very 'trendy'. I'm up against all these 'multimedia' subjects like . . . 'web design'. It's all about the future which, you know, is fine, obviously. Good. But I don't really get excited about video cameras getting smaller and iPods and getting onto level bloody 2067. No one really cares about all the stuff that's come before. History is . . .

PETA. People.

STEVEN. Sorry?

PETA. History's about people.

STEVEN. Exactly. Exactly that. History is about people. No one wants to know about people any more, unless they're in those celebrity magazines with their trousers hanging down. (*Beat.*) Everything's 'vocational' and that's bloody important, of course, obviously . . . but you know, you've got to . . . I don't know . . . reflect as well. I don't think there's anything wrong with that. I picked Latin over German when I was at school and I got a lot of stick. People saying Latin was bloody useless and what was I going to do with it and all that, but I'm glad I did it. I liked it. I thought it was good.

PETA. Would you feel better if I put this back as a proper couch?

STEVEN. No. Not at all. (*He leans on his side, supporting his head with his hand, desperately trying to look relaxed.*)

PETA. It's a day out though, innit?

STEVEN. Yes. Yeah. It's nice to get out for a change, even if the kids are arseholes. I just . . . I've got a . . . it's really daft, to be honest, but I've got a . . . thing about Hampton Court.

PETA. A thing?

STEVEN. It's stupid, really.

PETA. Go on.

STEVEN. It isn't so much to do with the place . . . I mean, it's beautiful. Ordinarily, I'd be more than bloody happy, get out of the classroom for a day . . . fresh air –

PETA. Go on.

STEVEN. It's a bit wet, really. I went there last year with my girlfriend . . . ex-girlfriend. We're not together any more.

PETA. I know what ex-girlfriend means.

STEVEN. Yeah. Yeah I –

PETA. Sorry.

STEVEN. No, it's fine, it's funny. Sarcasm. (*Pause.*) Erm, so what was I – Yeah, it was a surprise. Hampton Court. Not exactly a trip to Paris or anything, granted, but she liked it there. She liked going. We usually went to Tesco on a Saturday morning so I pretended we were – did the 'come on, let's go to Tesco' routine.

PETA. See, I like that, not too flash, but nice, thoughtful. She liked it there. No one's ever taken me somewhere cos I liked it, it's always been cos they liked it.

STEVEN. Yeah . . . well, anyway . . . she got angry when she realised we weren't actually going to Tesco because she had her tracksuit on and it was a warm day and she didn't have a T-shirt on underneath. She said I could have warned her to make an effort . . . but I said, you know . . . that would have spoilt the surprise. She just said it wasn't much of a surprise anyway.

PETA. Miserable cunt.

STEVEN. I think she felt bad when I got the picnic out. Things picked up a bit then. It was nice. We talked, y'know, nothing . . . I told all the things I didn't usually make time for . . . little things but important . . . stuff I needed to say . . . to let her know.

PETA. Like what?

STEVEN. Just things . . . little personal things.

PETA. Rude stuff?

STEVEN. No, not at all. Like . . . I don't know (*Long pause.*) She had this look. On her face. She did it sometimes. When we were on our own. Together. In bed. Not . . . just lying together. She couldn't do it if I asked her, it was just . . . I'd do it sometimes . . . practise it in the mirror when I was brushing my teeth . . . I couldn't ever do it like she did but that was why I loved it.

Pause.

Sorry . . . I don't want to go on, be boring –

PETA. I don't mind.

STEVEN. I told her I always shopped in my head for her . . . like 'she'd love that' or 'she'd look great in that' or how, when I spoke to people, I'd always judge them by her standards and I didn't tell her I loved her enough . . . all that stuff and other things . . . like really basic things that made me wonder what we did actually talk about. (*Pause.*) I'd never wanted to get married before, I've always been the first to go on about it being a piece of paper and not really meaning anything, but I'd started to think differently about it. Julie and I celebrating the fact that we loved each other . . . in front of all our mates. Y'know, just . . .

PETA. What did she say?

STEVEN. Nothing. For a while. Then she told me it was over. She'd met someone in work. Someone called Gary.

PETA. Bitch.

STEVEN. I'm making it sound worse than it was. She was very . . . she said we hadn't been right for a long time. That she loved me very much but it wasn't the same any more. She hadn't slept with this . . . Gary yet and it wasn't because of him . . . all the usual, you know –

PETA. Bollocks.

STEVEN. No, not . . . it was the stuff you say to ease it for the other person . . . how special we were together, how . . . love 'changes and evolves' . . . and 'what's being in love anyway?' and . . . you know . . . how – yes actually . . . complete fucking bollocks. (*Pause.*) She had the cheek to say I wasn't romantic . . . I said, 'What about today?' but she said it had come too late and she'd made her mind up. She needed other things . . . blah fucking blah. I told her how much I missed her when we apart and she said she never missed me because I never went anywhere . . . even when I was somewhere . . . or something, it didn't actually make any sense at all.

She wanted spontaneity, adventure . . . I said I can be spontaneous . . . I just need a little bit of time to plan, that's me and she said, 'Yes, that's you.' And I'd lost her. (*Pause.*) We sat in silence for ages . . . I couldn't leave, so I curled up in a ball with my head on her lap and stayed there. She kept trying to get me up at first but she gave in. We just stayed there. Eventually the man, the keeper with the leaf-stabber, came over and asked us to leave. He made some joke about young love. (*Pause.*) I wanted to get that fucking thing and impale him on it.

PETA. Have you ever seen *The Boston Strangler*?

STEVEN. No. Why?

PETA. Nothing. I just wondered. It was on telly the other night. Tony Curtis is the Boston Strangler, but you don't see him for ages to, like, keep you guessing. Anyway, he kills all these women.

STEVEN. Strangles them?

PETA. Obviously.

STEVEN. Yeah, 'course . . . he's the –

PETA. Anyway, you should think he's a complete fuckin' loon who got what he deserved, but you just can't help feeling really sorry for him.

STEVEN. It's a true story.

PETA. I know. Do you ever see her?

STEVEN. No.

PETA. Are you over it now?

STEVEN. Yeah, God. (*Pause.*) Yeah . . . don't even think about it any more. Don't even know where she is, but I hope she's well . . . I really do. Hope she's well.

PETA. I don't want all that . . . relationships. Too much. Had one . . . older than me, very . . . You don't need that, do you? Not at my age. Didn't need it.

STEVEN. She lives with him now, I think.

PETA. Didn't need the . . . volume. Not the noise . . . but the way everything changes around you. Like being deaf with the speakers on full blast. Thinking that you're shouting really fuckin' loud when you're just making shapes with your mouth. I got sick of me head ringing.

STEVEN. Yeah . . . but it's about dignity at the end of the day really, isn't it? I could go round shouting and kicking doors but where does that get you?

PETA. I don't know.

STEVEN. It was obviously time for us to move on. She just realised that first. That's the best way to think of it. She left this note when she moved out, at the top it said, 'Enclosed: Bits of my head for you to keep. I don't want them any more.' It wasn't even a letter really, it was more like a sort of . . . diary . . . about me. There was something so . . . final about that. Much more than her physically not being there. Giving back her thoughts along with all the CDs and books and crap. That made me . . . (*Pause.*) Sorry . . . I'm being really fucking boring now, aren't I? I haven't really talked about it, to be honest, since we split up . . . men don't, really, do they?

PETA. I don't know.

STEVEN. Maybe we should talk about other stuff.

PETA. I don't mind . . . talking about this. If you want to. I don't mind.

STEVEN. What are you studying?

Pause.

PETA. Fashion Design. I'm going to be a fashion designer . . . one day, like.

STEVEN. Wow . . . Great. So what –

PETA. Do you like being a teacher?

STEVEN. Most of the time . . . not always. What are your designs like?

PETA. Do you shout?

STEVEN. Not half as much as I should . . . No, I try not to. It just doesn't work. Some people think it does but I've never found that to be the case, I think it's more about –

PETA. I knew you were a teacher.

STEVEN. Did you?

PETA. You look like one. In a good way. You look thoughtful. Do they fancy yer? The girls?

STEVEN. Erm . . . no, I don't think –

PETA. I bet they do. If you're under thirty-odd and you're not in, like, Elephant-Man league you always get some fancy yer. It's not always because they really do, sometimes it's just cos you're showing an interest in them. Treating them like proper people. They look up to you. I fell in love with me Maths teacher once because he asked me if everything was OK at home, and I hate maths . . . really shit at it . . . and he was nothing to look at.

STEVEN. Right.

PETA. But you're nice . . . I bet there's loads.

STEVEN. Not that I notice.

PETA. How old are you?

STEVEN. Twenty-nine . . . thirty next month.

PETA. How old do you think I am?

STEVEN. Oh I don't know, I'm rubbish at stuff like that . . . I always offend people. I've got no idea.

PETA. Oh come on . . . just guess . . . you won't offend me . . . it's not like I'm fifty and I want to you say I look twenty . . . go 'ead.

STEVEN. Eighteen.

PETA. Twenty.

STEVEN. You look younger.

PETA. People always say I look dead young . . . that's why I asked you to guess. I still can't get served sometimes. Have you got a girlfriend?

STEVEN. No . . . if I was, well, I wouldn't be here, would I?

PETA. I don't know.

STEVEN. Well, I wouldn't . . . I don't think I could live with myself –

PETA. You're a bit serious, you, aren't yer?

STEVEN. I'm just . . . it's just the way I am.

PETA. Good for you.

STEVEN. It's not very – (*Pulls a face.*) – Is it though?

PETA. Very what?

STEVEN. Y'know, very . . . (*Pulls same face.*)

PETA. I don't know what you're on about.

STEVEN. Sorry yeah . . . I mean. It isn't very . . . people these days have very different ideas about relationships. Commitment. They all just a bit . . . (*Pulls the face again.*)

PETA. Can you pack that face thing in?

STEVEN. Sorry. People are lax, aren't they? About it all. I mean, I've got one friend, one friend out of . . . all my friends, who has never been unfaithful to a girlfriend. Never had even a one-night stand or anything. I think that's . . . that's why, when you said, 'Have you got a girlfriend?', I was just a bit –

PETA. Hold on. Just because I invited you in doesn't mean I'm up for it, yer know.

STEVEN. Sorry, no, I didn't presume anything, it's just –

PETA. Just what?

STEVEN. Just. Well, I'm here, aren't I?

PETA. And –

STEVEN. I don't know.

PETA. Don't yer? Well, know this, I don't make a habit of this inviting blokes I don't know back to me flat. I thought you seemed nice . . . felt sorry for yer, out on your own. You're a teacher.

STEVEN. You were on your own.

PETA. Don't change the subject.

STEVEN. I'm not, I'm just saying that –

PETA. Man out on his own looks a bit weird if yer ask me . . . thinking about it now, like, dunno what I was thinking of. Girl on her own's OK . . . not likely to be some pervert, am I?

Pause.

STEVEN. I think I'd best go then, thanks for . . .

Pause.

PETA. I don't think yer weird.

STEVEN. OK but –

PETA. I was just . . . making a point. You shouldn't make assumptions, jump to conclusions.

STEVEN. Point taken. Sorry if I offen –

PETA. Don't worry about it. Don't get a cob on.

STEVEN. I haven't got a 'cob on'. It's just I –

PETA. You have a bit.

STEVEN. I just . . . I'd hate to think –

PETA. I don't think anything. Sorry.

STEVEN. I just wanted to see what it was like, really. People don't notice you're on your own when it's a big club like that, do they? I sort of bypassed all that when I was younger – head in a book most of the time, few pints somewhere quiet. Didn't really do the whole . . . ravey thing.

PETA. Ravey?

STEVEN. I had been with people. Couple of fellas I got friendly with through work. Went to The Crown and Two Chairmen in Covent Garden with them. Nice . . . nice blokes. But they're married, you know, so . . . last orders and they're off back home to their families. People are waiting for them somewhere. And I'm a bit pissed and I think . . . why not go on somewhere anyway. What's the big deal? Nobody's waiting for me anywhere. Go and . . . you know –

PETA. Pick up a young bird and see if yer can get into her knickers.

STEVEN. No . . . not at all. Now see –

PETA. Right . . . sorry I'm just being . . .

STEVEN. I'm not . . . I mean, you're really attractive, of course . . . I wouldn't be here if . . . I'm not the most confident of men. I'm not great with women, girls . . . whatever. Never have been really, always just making a bit of a hash of things but then I met Julie and for some bizarre reason, she seemed to think I'd do and then . . . I got found out. Knew it would happen I suppose but it still gets you, right in there. Truth is . . . I don't know . . . It's hard to know what to say. I'm a bit out of touch, I've never really been that in touch to be honest . . . it's all . . . well, I don't find it easy, Peta. A year down the line and I'm fine but all this preliminary stuff . . .

PETA. You're too serious.

STEVEN. It's a serious business.

PETA. What is?

STEVEN. Love.

PETA. See –

STEVEN. I'm just not very . . . confident.

PETA. Confidence has got nothing to do with love, being good at chatting up girls has got fuck all to do with love.

STEVEN. That's not at all what I'm trying to say . . . I'm just pointing out that I'm . . . I find it hard. Any of it. I don't feel like a very capable or decent person at the best of times so I don't know how I'm supposed to persuade anyone that I'm . . . you know, capable of being with them. (*Beat.*) I should be asking you what music you like. I sound like a complete tosser and I'm not . . . not really.

Pause.

PETA. No . . . you're not.

STEVEN. Thanks.

PETA. You just think too much. I do too. You need to keep a lid on that.

STEVEN. I'm a bit more sober than I thought I was . . .

PETA. There's an all-night offy five minutes down the road. You could nip out. Get a bottle. I could come with yer, if yer wanted.

STEVEN. I don't know –

PETA. You don't have to. It's good . . . talking to yer.

STEVEN. I should get going really . . . up early tomorrow.

PETA. You don't have to.

STEVEN. No . . . it's fine –

PETA. I know it's gone a bit . . . weird but I think you're OK,
I didn't mean to be arsey . . . I just –

STEVEN. It isn't because of that. I do understand but . . . it's
really late –

PETA. That's just me.

STEVEN. Yes. No, it's fine . . . there's absolutely no –

PETA. You don't have to, you know . . . no funny business and
that but you don't have to. We could top and tail. I think
you're sound.

STEVEN. I don't . . . no, I think it might be best if I just went
home.

PETA. The tubes have stopped.

STEVEN. I'll get the night bus.

PETA. To Colliers Wood? You'll get four, more like.

STEVEN. I . . . how long do you think it'll take?

PETA. Dunno . . . two hours if you're lucky.

STEVEN. Oh Christ –

PETA. I've got a spare duvet there . . . we can have one each.

STEVEN. Really, I don't –

PETA. Lighten up. You need some new experiences, you . . .
that's what's wrong with you. The same things don't happen
twice, that can be good or bad depending on how you look
at it. My glass is half-full, Steven, I think it's good to be
like that. Maybe it's because you know too much . . . all
that stuff. History's all about killing and dying, isn't it? It's
enough to make anyone a bit too serious.

Long pause.

I know what you mean . . . what you meant before. About saying things or not saying things or wanting to – that's all I do. Ever. It's hard being honest about stuff.

STEVEN. It is, yeah.

PETA. Sorry for –

STEVEN. You've got absolutely nothing to be sorry about.

PETA. I know. I didn't even mean sorry. I'm not really sure I know what it means. I say it if there's a gap. Some silence.

Pause.

Sorry. See –

STEVEN. Have you got an alarm?

PETA (*brightly*). Yeah.

STEVEN. Can I use the bathroom?

PETA. 'Course you can.

STEVEN goes into the bathroom while PETA changes into a pair of pyjamas she's pulled from her chest of drawers. She pulls another duvet from under the sofa bed and starts making two separate little places with pillows at either end. She gets two glasses of water from the kitchen, also putting them at either end of the bed, then sets the small alarm clock on top of the chest. She picks the photo up and looks at it. STEVEN comes out of the bathroom, she sets it back down.

start section 2

STEVEN. Who's that?

PETA. Me dad. Should turn him round . . . he wouldn't be happy.

STEVEN. Would he disapprove?

PETA. Catholic.

STEVEN. Even topping and tailing?

PETA. Oh yeah. He'd have your guts for garters.

STEVEN. Is he likely to come around?

PETA. Hardly (*She dives into the bed, pulling the covers around her.*) Are you just gonna stand there all night or what?

STEVEN. Should I just . . . ?

PETA. Get in, yeah . . . I've put you down there, is that OK?

STEVEN. Yes . . . fine . . . thanks.

He clambers in fully dressed.

PETA. Aren't you gonna take your kecks off?

STEVEN. I'm fine.

PETA. I won't be offended by yer in your undies.

STEVEN. Honestly . . . I'd rather just leave them on.

PETA. They're a bit tweedy . . . can you watch them rubbing against me leg?

STEVEN. Yes.

PETA. The light switch's on the wall above you . . . to your left . . . when you're ready.

STEVEN. Right, thanks . . . do you want to read or anything?

PETA. No.

STEVEN. Right . . . should I just –

PETA. If you want . . . I've put the alarm down there for you.

STEVEN. Oh yes . . . thanks.

He picks it up and sets it.

PETA. What time will you have to get up?

STEVEN. Erm . . . six, I suppose . . . be on the safe side . . . (*Leans up to the light.*) Can I?

PETA. Go for it.

He switches the light off. They lie in silence in the dark for a few moments.

I hate the dark.

No reply.

Do you?

Pause.

STEVEN. Sorry?

She clambers out of bed and switches the light back on, before getting back in.

PETA. Hate the dark. Do you?

STEVEN. Erm . . . no . . . not really.

PETA. I get scared. (*Pause.*) I always imagine I can see things . . . faces. Monsters . . . it's daft, that, isn't it? The weird thing is, as a little kid, I wasn't like that at all . . . you get told all the time, don't yer? There's nothing to be frightened of. Then you get older and you realise there's fucking everything to be frightened of.

STEVEN. Lots of people . . . adults . . . are scared of the dark. I think there's a name for it.

PETA. Yeah, I think it's called Life.

STEVEN. I meant –

PETA. I know what you meant. Do you mind . . . five more minutes?

STEVEN. No . . . no, fine.

Pause.

PETA. I'm not in college tomorrow . . . I'm off. Day to meself.

STEVEN. Lucky you.

PETA. Don't know what I'm going to do.

STEVEN. Haven't you got lots of coursework?

PETA. Finished me projects.

STEVEN. You should have showed me what you've been doing.

PETA. They're all in college . . . getting marked.

STEVEN. Oh.

Long pause.

PETA. Could I come?

STEVEN. Sorry?

PETA. Could I come on the trip tomorrow? To Hampton Court.

STEVEN. Erm . . . well, I don't know . . . I don't think –

PETA. It doesn't matter.

STEVEN. It's just that . . . well . . . it might seem a bit odd.

PETA. What might?

STEVEN. Turning up in the same clothes as yesterday . . .
   with a strange girl.

PETA. Cheers.

STEVEN. You know what I mean . . . surely –

PETA. Teachers always wear the same clothes and you could
   say I was your friend. I could be a helper. You don't have to
   let on you met me the night before, do yer?

STEVEN. No, but even so . . . I just don't think it's a good
   idea.

PETA. OK.

STEVEN. Sorry.

PETA. It's alright . . . honestly, don't worry about it.

STEVEN. I mean, we could . . . always . . . we could go
   another time if you wanted to.

PETA. Hampton Court?

STEVEN. No. Wherever –

PETA. I don't really fancy that, to be honest. Henry the
   Eighth's put me off.

STEVEN. No, well . . . wherever, we could go for a drink or –

PETA. I quite fancy the aquarium. My dad took me to London
   once. Just for a day. We went to the aquarium. That's why

I moved down. Not because of the aquarium but the whole day. London.

STEVEN. Right –

PETA. Would you want to go the aquarium?

STEVEN. Yes . . . yes, that would be fine . . . if you liked.

PETA. They've got sharks too.

STEVEN. Yeah . . . they have. They're only small though . . . you can get in with them apparently.

PETA. Fuck that. Would it be a date?

STEVEN. Erm . . . I don't know really.

PETA. Do you fancy me then?

STEVEN. Sorry?

PETA. You're saying you fancy me?

STEVEN. Not 'fancy', it's not . . . well, yes, I mean. I wouldn't be here, would I, if I didn't find you interesting and attractive. It's just . . . difficult, isn't it?

PETA. What is?

STEVEN. Meeting people. Being honest.

PETA. I s'pose so.

STEVEN. Connecting.

PETA. Yeah.

STEVEN. I sound like a tosser, don't I?

PETA. No. Would you stroke my head? Just for a minute. Nothing funny . . . just 'til I'm asleep.

STEVEN. Erm . . . yes if you, erm –

PETA. I'll get down your end.

She wriggles under the covers to STEVEN's end of the bed.

I can get back up there when you're done, if you want.

He starts to stroke her head awkwardly, putting one leg on the floor.

STEVEN. Is that right?

PETA. S'nice, yeah.

Pause.

STEVEN. I feel like . . . I sound like some lonely fucked-up emotional mess. And, you know . . . I'm not. I have a very loyal group of about six friends from university, all based in London who I see regularly and old school friends from home who I ring whenever I'm in Berkhamstead at my parents . . . plus a couple of people at work who I've become quite close to. Admittedly, I haven't had full sex since Julie, but I have taken a couple of women out casually for drinks and just not been really interested . . . you know . . . so . . . I'm not a complete . . . fucking . . . loser or . . . whatever you must think. I'd just had a bad day. I don't think I'm incompetent . . . I think I've got a lot to offer. I'm just . . . fucking look at me, it's ridiculous. (*Pause.*) I heard this thing the other day . . . I read this thing . . . that someone had written. They said that battle-fear and love-sickness are the same. I completely get that. I really do.

Pause.

PETA (*sleepily*). Aren't you tired yet?

STEVEN. Not really but I'll . . .

He reaches up and switches the light off, before settling back under the covers.

PETA. Makes you tired. I'm dropping off. Me dad used to stroke me hair, when I was little . . . just stroke me head . . . it'd send me off to sleep in about two seconds flat. It's nice . . . having your head stroked.

STEVEN. We had a dog, a Border Collie called Tina. I used to stroke her. Although I don't suppose that counts really, does it?

PETA. Yeah. Same difference. Comfort. S'good for yer, isn't it? Stroking yer pets. Therapeutic.

STEVEN. She ate her pups.

PETA. For fuck's sake.

STEVEN. Only because she thought they were in danger. It was fucking . . . horrible. At the time. When we were kids. It isn't what you expect, is it? Scared the living daylights . . . but now there's something quite . . . beautiful about it. Does that sound really . . . ? I never stroked her again after that and then she died. I haven't thought about that for years. She used to try and jump up on my knee and I wouldn't let her because she ate her pups. It made me feel sick. But she was only doing what she thought was best. That makes me feel a bit sad now.

Pause.

Peta?

PETA (*half-asleep*). You've got to get up in four hours.

STEVEN. Yeah. Hampton bloody Court.

He continues to stroke her head for a minute or so before gently prising himself away. In the half-light we can just make him out, gathering his things together. Quietly he lets himself out, pulling the door behind him, almost silently. When he has gone, PETA *sits up straight away.*

Blackout.

Scene Three

Lights up. It is morning. PETA *is on her mobile.*

PETA. It's not working. (*Pause.*) Because I'm not getting any messages. I keep it off a lot of the time. (*Pause.*) I can't. (*Pause.*) Because I'm a librarian. (*Pause.*) When I switch it on, there's no messages. There should be . . . OK. Yeah, alright.

PETA *switches the phone off. The sound of vomiting can be heard from the bathroom. She listens at the door.*

Are you OK?

No reply. PETA *switches the phone back on. It bleeps; there is a message. She listens.*

CHANTELLE *staggers out of the bathroom and clutches onto the chest of drawers.* PETA *turns the phone off quickly.*

CHANTELLE. Fuckin' hell.

PETA*'s phone rings. She answers.* CHANTELLE *sprawls on the bed.*

PETA. Hello . . . I got it just then, yeah . . . yeah. Ta. (*She ends the call.*) Tosser.

CHANTELLE. Fella?

PETA. Some useless Orange twat.

CHANTELLE. Eh?

PETA. Me phone's broke. I don't get messages.

CHANTELLE. Maybe no one's ringing yer.

Silence.

PETA. D'yer reckon that's the last of it now?

CHANTELLE. Jesus, I fuckin' hope so.

PETA. Do you feel any better?

CHANTELLE. No. I feel worse.

PETA. Do you want some water?

CHANTELLE. I've had three pints . . . it just shoots straight back out. I'm like a fountain. You could stick a fucking jug on me head and put me in the middle of Trafalgar Square.

PETA *comes and sits on the bed.*

I got a bit on your bathroom floor . . . I'll clean it up in a minute.

PETA. It doesn't matter . . . do you want some toast?

CHANTELLE *makes a baulking noise. Pause.*

I feel fine.

CHANTELLE. Fuckin' good for you.

Pause.

Sorry.

PETA. S'alright.

CHANTELLE. S'me own fault.

PETA. I hate being sick.

CHANTELLE. Self-inflicted . . . you shouldn't be so nice.

PETA. Even so . . . it's still shit.

CHANTELLE. Yeah.

PETA. You were bladdered.

CHANTELLE. I made a right twat of myself, didn't I?

PETA. No. Just pissed. Same as everyone else.

PETA *goes over to the chair where* CHANTELLE's *clothes are strewn. She picks up a tiny sparkly top and holds it against herself, then notices a pair of pointy, really high turquoise shoes on the floor. She slips them on.*

You've got nice clothes.

She notices a chunky plastic bracelet and slips that on too.

Nice things.

CHANTELLE. Cheers. Oh God . . . I think my head's going to explode.

PETA. Do you want a tablet?

CHANTELLE. I found some Ibuprofen in the kitchen . . . I've had six.

PETA. They're strong, them . . . you could kill yourself.

CHANTELLE. Good. I wish I was fucking dead.

PETA. Anyone else would have done the same.

CHANTELLE. No, they wouldn't.

PETA. They would. I would.

CHANTELLE. Would yer?

PETA. Too right.

CHANTELLE. You're just being nice.

PETA. He was a prick. He deserved it.

CHANTELLE. He was . . . *is* a fuckin' prick but still –

PETA. He was getting off with a girl . . . on a night out with you –

CHANTELLE. I know, but I could have dealt with it a bit different, couldn't I? My mum always says, 'Never let them think you give a fuck, Chantelle. Keep your cool and you keep your dignity.'

PETA. You did. Sort of.

CHANTELLE. Where's the fucking dignity in throwing an ashtray at someone's head?

PETA. It didn't hit him.

CHANTELLE. More's the fuckin' pity. (*Pause.*) I dunno, I mean, I've only been seeing him a month . . . it's hardly betrayal of the century, is it?

PETA. You said he told yer he loved yer.

CHANTELLE. He did.

PETA. Well, he's a prick.

CHANTELLE. Yeah.

PETA. You deserve better.

CHANTELLE. Yeah. Thanks for all that. You're a proper diamond. (*Pause.*) Listen, this is gonna sound really bad but . . . I've forgotten your name.

PETA. Peta.

CHANTELLE. Peta . . . 'course yeah, sorry babe. (*Beat.*) Isn't that a bloke's name?

PETA. If you're a bloke . . . it's spelt with an 'a' instead of 'e-r'.

CHANTELLE. Right. Unusual, that.

PETA. I think me mum made it up to be honest.

CHANTELLE. No . . . I wasn't being funny . . . It's nice, I really like it. I'm Chantelle.

PETA. I know, you said.

CHANTELLE. About five times probably.

PETA. Something like that.

CHANTELLE. Oh well . . . you're a diamond anyway. I dread to think what I might have done next, if you hadn't come over.

PETA. Not a lot probably, the bouncers chucked you out pretty much straight away.

CHANTELLE. Shit, yeah . . . oh it gets worse. You didn't have to leave with me though . . . I can't believe I wrecked your night as well.

PETA. It's fine, honest . . . I wasn't having such a great time anyway . . . I was with me mate and she copped off with some bloke, buggered off and left me on my own.

CHANTELLE. See, I hate girls like that . . . no sense of comradeship.

PETA. How's your ankle?

CHANTELLE. Why, what happened?

PETA. You fell over outside, don't you remember? Said you thought you'd twisted it.

CHANTELLE. Fuck yeah. Oh God, he didn't see, did he? Fucking cherry on the cake that'd be.

PETA. No one saw. Only me.

CHANTELLE. I am never drinking again. Ever.

PETA. Right.

CHANTELLE. I'm fuckin' serious. Well, not 'ever' but I definitely need a little chat with myself. Sort a few things out. Woman to woman.

PETA. Are you sad . . . about him, like?

CHANTELLE. Nah . . . latest in a long line of losers . . .
I don't know how I attract them, but fuckin' hell do I ever.
I must have a funny, simple look on me face . . . one of me
mates actually said that to me once, can you get onto that?
She goes, 'Channy, you've got "take the piss" written all
over you.' I had a right moody on with her but I'm starting
to think she might be right. They get me though, every time
they get me. Look at this. (*She roots around in her handbag
which has been cast aside on the floor. She pulls out a
letter.*) Now this . . . this is what he wrote to me last week.
Thursday.

PETA. What is it?

CHANTELLE. It's a letter.

PETA. A love letter?

CHANTELLE. Well . . . yeah, s'what I thought, I mean, it's
dressed up like that and everything . . . read the end though.

PETA (*struggling to read*). 'See you next' –

CHANTELLE. No . . . the very end bit . . . where he signs it.

PETA. 'Love, Gary'?

CHANTELLE. Yeah, that.

PETA. 'Love, Gary.'

CHANTELLE. Yeah.

PETA. That's . . . nice, isn't it?

CHANTELLE. No . . . it ain't . . . he's spelt it 'l-u-v'. That's
crap.

PETA. It's still love. Love from Gary. He could have just put
'Gary'.

CHANTELLE. I'd rather he had done, just 'Gary' would have
been . . . enigmatic. 'L-u-v' is fucking, well, s-h-i-t.

PETA. In that song . . . what is it? By like The Chiffons or The
Shirelles or something, dead old sixties one anyway, they

go, 'When I say I'm in love you'd best believe I'm in love –
l-u-v.' That's a proper love song.

CHANTELLE. No, it ain't . . . it's a pop song for stupid little
sixties teenagers who weren't allowed to do anything, you
wouldn't get Kate Bush writing about l-u-v.

PETA. He's northern, isn't he?

CHANTELLE. Leeds.

PETA. There you go . . . that's how they say love. 'Luv.'

CHANTELLE. 'Whatever' now anyway, innit?

PETA. It's not you, it's blokes, they're mental . . . knobheads,
the lot of them.

CHANTELLE. Yeah. You got a fella?

PETA. I did have but we split up.

CHANTELLE. Sorry darlin' . . . when was this?

PETA. Few months ago . . . that's why I moved down really,
just to get away from it . . . couldn't face seeing him . . . it
cracked me up.

CHANTELLE. He break your heart?

PETA. I think I broke his. He still calls. He made me head
ring. I couldn't . . . it was hard to get away. That's his
picture up there. Don't know why I put it up but –

CHANTELLE. You just did. You just do though, don't you?
It's hard . . . I've been there more times than I can
remember now. Like water off a duck's back. He's
handsome, in' he?

PETA. I miss him . . . I miss what I thought he was. That was
too long ago now though. Different life. He's a history
teacher. He's dead clever. I wanted to marry him and have
babies once.

CHANTELLE. Bit young for that, ain't yer?

PETA. Yeah. That's what I thought. In the end. Wanted to do
things. See things. I feel like –

CHANTELLE. He don't look like a teacher. I'm not saying he doesn't look clever. He just doesn't look . . . like a teacher. Is that bad, saying that?

PETA. No.

CHANTELLE. He doesn't though, does he? You been out with anyone since? Anyone down here?

PETA. No . . . I just . . . nah . . . I haven't met anyone decent.

CHANTELLE. We should get ourselves out, girl . . . you should witness me in a better state than I was last night . . . I can be a right laugh.

PETA. Yeah . . . defo, that'd be good.

CHANTELLE. Could you do us a favour and pass my bag over?

PETA *passes* CHANTELLE*'s bag – another sparkly number.* CHANTELLE *roots around, pulling out various items of make-up; lipstick, concealer, compact.* PETA *watches with interest as she starts putting it on.*

Jesus, I don't think Polyfilla'd do it today. Look at the fuckin' state of me. No wonder he wanted to shag someone else.

PETA. What's that?

CHANTELLE. It's called 'Luminesse'. It's meant to . . . 'accentuate and define your cheekbones'. I think it makes me look a bit like Metal Mickey, but there you go. If it costs more than twenty quid, you think it's gonna change your life, don't you?

PETA. It's nice. (*Beat.*) Could I have a go?

CHANTELLE. Help yourself.

CHANTELLE *hands the tube over.* PETA *takes it and squeezes a bit onto her hand.*

PETA. Is that enough? Do I just –

CHANTELLE. Stick it on, yeah. Rub it in properly . . . I put it on me eyelids too, when I'm going out.

PETA *starts rubbing it onto her cheeks and eyes. Without any other make-up, the result is a bit odd-looking.*

PETA. Is that it?

Pause.

CHANTELLE. Yeah . . . yeah, I mean, usually you might have a bit of lippy or something as well. Eyeliner, bit of mascara.

PETA. I haven't got much make-up really.

CHANTELLE. You don't need it. Now looking at this face . . . fucking hell, I think plastic surgery's the only way forward. God, I keep getting the most horrendous fucking flashbacks. Why do I do it to myself?

PETA. You just got drunk. People get drunk.

CHANTELLE. It's gin what does it. Give me vodka and I'm wicked as . . . could drink it in buckets. Gin, work of the devil, turns me into a freak. You wanna get me on a vodka night, Peta.

PETA. I like vodka.

CHANTELLE (*imitating her accent*). 'I like vodka.'

Silence.

Sorry, I bet you get that all the fucking time, don't yer?

PETA. Not really. Where d'yer go . . . when you go out?

CHANTELLE. Depends. Have me little phases. We usually have a laugh though . . . wherever. (*Pause.*) You should come out. Meet the girls, you'd like them, I reckon.

PETA. Yeah . . . that'd be good.

CHANTELLE. What you doin' down here anyway?

PETA. How d'yer mean?

CHANTELLE. What d'yer do? You got a job?

PETA. I'm looking at the moment . . . I just left somewhere, temping but they took me on permanent. It was awful . . . dead boring, I was a dogsbody.

CHANTELLE. Where was that?

PETA. Some crap place . . . call centre. I'm looking now, something a bit different . . . something else, work with some nice people. In an office . . . have a bit of a laugh. What's your office like?

CHANTELLE. Fuckin' shit. About as funny as AIDS. You don't want to even think about it. Turns me head to mush. Can't wanna work in an office . . . What do you really want to do?

PETA. I'm not sure . . . loads . . . everything really. Change me mind all the time, I want to do something that makes people ask questions, do you know what I mean? Makes me feel proud. I'm fed up of being the one who does all the asking.

CHANTELLE. I'm a nosey bitch, me . . . never get fed up of asking . . . How do you afford it, living here on your own?

PETA. Well, I won't for much longer if I don't get meself sorted . . . it's a shithole anyway.

CHANTELLE. Yeah, but living on your own . . . expensive that is . . . I'd give anything to live on my own. I'm still with me mum and dad . . . can you believe it? S'fucking well embarrassing that is . . .

PETA. That wouldn't be so bad . . . gets lonely on your own.

CHANTELLE. No, it doesn't . . . it gets lonely if you're with the wrong people, that's what happens. Put me on me own, I'd be fine I reckon. I'm best on my own . . . I always forget that. I want to do things but I'm not sure what they are. I'm not in the right environment. I need to get together with people who do stuff. Or not at all. Fuck everyone off.

PETA. I'm not good on me own.

CHANTELLE. I think sometimes, I wonder what's gonna happen next. In my life. What is gonna happen? Then I see myself. In a few years time. Exactly the same as now . . . no different. Just a different sad arse, making a fool out of me.

PETA. Don't you want kids?

CHANTELLE. Can't see it. (*Pause.*) Could have, though. I got pregnant once. You ever got pregnant, Peta?

Pause.

PETA. No.

CHANTELLE. I have.

Silence.

I don't mind talking about it. I don't regret it. The day I found out I was freaked at first, obviously, did a test on me own and it didn't really sink in, to be honest . . . you don't feel any different. Not that you would, your body and stuff . . . but mentally . . . I didn't feel any different, I just thought how mad's that? My mate's got a little boy and she reckons she, well, knew before she did a test, she goes, 'Oh you just know, Chan, you feel different, like you see things in a new way . . . ' Well, I think that's bollocks. Anyway, I thought I'd treat meself . . . celebrate. Joke, obviously. I went to this little French restaurant in Clapham for lunch, really expensive. Top-notch place . . . really romantic. I thought I'll get all the best things on the menu . . . write a dodgy cheque for it. Make the most of a surreal day. I sat down and I started watching this couple at a table by the window and they were obviously together, together but you've never seen anything so wrong in all your life . . . not like they were ugly or nothing, they just didn't . . . you could tell for a start that they were bound to split up.

PETA. How d'yer tell that?

CHANTELLE. She had hold of his hand, oblivious to everything else and he's somewhere else entirely and I could hear what they're saying and it wasn't anything like I bet they wanted to say. All polite and clipped. Then they get the bill and she stands up first to leave and she's pregnant and I thought, 'Jesus, that's you done now, love.' Scared the living daylights out of me. Not that I needed anything else to help make me mind up but I thought some things are so not right . . . do you know what I mean?

PETA. Do you regret doing it . . . do you ever think –

CHANTELLE. Sometimes I get sad. Not about that specifically but it's there, like . . . a layer. I get sad, but I don't really ever seem it, so nobody asks and I get pissed off with 'em all. Like, feel really lonely and that's my fault really, isn't it? My mum's always on at me . . . worrying.

PETA. It's good . . . that's good for someone to worry about yer.

CHANTELLE. I think she's selfish. I said to her the other week, 'Do you worry about me?' I mean, that's a stupid question but it's not such a stupid question actually. 'Apart from being run over or raped or mugged or murdered . . . or fucking getting pregnant. Do you actually worry about me? Do you worry about my head?' and she said, 'What's wrong with your head?' and I said, 'I don't know, nothing . . . it just . . . ' and I couldn't explain. I never can really, I'm shit at it. Can't really be arsed once I've opened me mouth. But I've opened up a whole new section of worry for her now. She wants me to go for a head scan. She's selfish. She's thinking about herself . . . without me. She doesn't imagine I might lose it . . . have a fuckin' breakdown, does she? Cos that wouldn't be so bad . . . she could have me at home all the time watching fuckin' *Trisha* with her.

PETA. Do you think you'll have a breakdown?

CHANTELLE. Nah. S'not the point though, is it? She doesn't know that. (*Beat.*) I sound like a bitch, don't I? She's OK really . . . a good girl. She just doesn't know me. How about you?

PETA. How about me what?

CHANTELLE. Dunno. All that shit . . . family rubbish.

PETA. Not much to say, really.

CHANTELLE. Never is, is there? Can't live with 'em, can't shoot 'em. Same goes for fellas.

PETA. What are you doing today?

CHANTELLE. I haven't thought that far ahead yet . . . I'm just contemplating vomiting again.

PETA. I'm gonna go out . . . into town. Do you want to come?

CHANTELLE. Might be a little bit ambitious that . . . where you going?

PETA. I fancy the aquarium . . . I've never been. Do you fancy that? It'd be good if you've got a hangover. It's dead . . . calm.

CHANTELLE. Oh I dunno . . . what about all those tiny little ones that dart about all over the shop, nothing fucking calming about them.

PETA. They've got a shark.

CHANTELLE. Are they good for hangovers n'all?

PETA. It'll take your mind off it.

CHANTELLE. No, ta. I'm going to go home, stick me head under the covers and come out when it's dark again.

PETA. Daytime doesn't let you get away with much, does it?

CHANTELLE *stands and starts getting all her stuff together from the night before.* PETA *sits watching on the bed.*

CHANTELLE (*scribbling her number down on a scrap of paper*). Thanks Peta, seriously . . . you give me a ring and we can go out for a drink sometime . . . meet the girls. It'd be a laugh.

PETA. Definitely. (*She takes the bracelet off her wrist and offers it to* CHANTELLE.) Here y'are.

CHANTELLE. You can have that if you like it.

PETA. Oh no . . . it's yours . . . I wasn't trying to –

CHANTELLE. Oh shut up. It was a fiver from Topshop. You said you liked it. Keep it. Least I can do, innit?

PETA. Thanks.

CHANTELLE. Tube far?

PETA. There's a bus stop just outside . . . just need to pull both doors to.

CHANTELLE. Right. See ya then.

PETA. See yer.

CHANTELLE *comes over and they hug awkwardly.*

CHANTELLE. Cheers.

PETA. Bye.

CHANTELLE *pulls the door shut behind her. PETA sits on the edge of the bed, feet on the floor, hands in her lap, head down. She spots something on the floor; CHANTELLE has left her cardigan – it's pink with sequins around the neck and cuffs. PETA puts it on. She goes into the bathroom. Looks in the mirror, comes out and takes it off, carefully folding and placing it in one of the drawers. She takes off the bangle and puts it on top of the cardigan before shutting the drawer. After a few seconds she gets her mobile from her bag and dials a number. She listens. It clicks straight to answerphone. She presses the red button. Redials. Presses the red button. She does this three times before throwing it onto the floor. She curls up in a foetus position on the bed for a few seconds before getting up and crawling under the bed. She surfaces, clutching some bits of paper. She finds a phone number and picking the phone back up from the floor, dials.*

Hello . . . Yeah, I called before. I tried . . . I've got an appointment but I missed . . . I wasn't sure of the date you gave me . . . Peta Sheldon . . . with an 'a' . . . No, Peta with an 'a', not Sheldon . . . Sheldon with an 'o'. (*Pause.*) The woman last time when I phoned . . . she went to speak to the nurse. She said, 'The line might go quiet but I haven't cut yer off.' I got cut off. I need . . . (*Pause.*) Yeah, I can hold on.

Blackout.

Scene Four

PETA *is lying under the covers on the sofa bed, curled up, her back towards us, her hair sticking out of the top of the covers. MARION is in the kitchen, out of view, moving around. After a few seconds, she walks into the living room, a lit cigarette in her hand. She sits on the edge of the bed, smoking, as she does throughout the scene. She is wearing checked pyjamas and a pink towelling dressing gown. She peers at PETA, checking her, pulling the covers around her. She sits in silence for a few moments before humming a song to herself. PETA stirs.*

MARION. Peta?

PETA *turns in her sleep.* MARION *shakes her gently.*

You alright, love? Peta? You alright?

Pause.

Peta? You awake now?

PETA *doesn't respond.* MARION *gets up and goes into the kitchen. She fetches a glass of milk and brings it in. Sitting on the side next to PETA, she lifts PETA's head and tries to get her to drink the milk.* PETA *wakes up properly and brushes her off. She sits up, staring ahead for a while.*

How you feeling?

Pause.

Crap probably, eh?

Pause.

Do you feel like crap? You probably will. That's alright. You'll probably feel like shit for a while and then you'll feel a bit better and then you'll feel fine. Just takes a bit . . . of time. Wouldn't be a bad thing to get you looked at, though.

Pause.

PETA. Were you talking to me?

MARION. When?

PETA. Just then.

MARION. Yeah . . . I was asking . . . how you're feeling.

PETA. Before that. Singing as well. I could hear it in me
    dream.

MARION. Could you? Bet that spoilt it. Bet it was nice up 'til
    then.

PETA. No.

MARION. I didn't want to fall asleep. I've been sat here hours.
    When I don't want to fall asleep, I do that . . . sing or talk to
    myself. Get locked up one of these days. Silly cow. You
    should have some milk. Put a lining on your stomach.
    (*Pause.*) Do you remember?

PETA. What?

MARION. Know who I am?

PETA. Yeah.

MARION. I'm Marion.

PETA. Yeah.

MARION. I live in the flat downstairs.

PETA. I know.

MARION. I helped you in. You were a bit pissed . . . you fell
    down the stairs.

    Silence.

    You were upset. You fell down –

PETA. I know. I remember.

    Pause.

MARION. I didn't want to leave you in case you were sick and
    choked on it.

PETA. Thanks.

MARION. It's OK.

    Pause.

I wanted to get you looked at. Get a doctor. I think maybe we still should –

PETA. I'm alright. I feel better.

MARION. You don't look better. You look dreadful. Could you eat something?

PETA. No. Thanks.

MARION. Do you mind me smoking? I shouldn't be . . . I just got a fright. You falling like that. Sounded like a . . . you can break your neck falling like that. I think you should see someone. I'd never forgive meself.

PETA. I've just got a headache.

MARION. Might be concussion.

PETA. I didn't bang it.

MARION. You gave me such a bloody fright.

PETA. Sorry.

MARION. It's OK. I'm not telling you off. It's none of my business. Just want to make sure you're OK.

PETA. Did I wake you up?

MARION. I wasn't asleep. But you bloody would have done if I was. Thought a baby elephant had fallen down the stairs. Thought someone was bloody ram-raiding the place.

PETA. Sorry.

MARION. You don't need to say sorry. You didn't throw yourself down them on purpose. (*Beat.*) Did you?

PETA. No. I never.

MARION. Just asking. I've got to ask. I don't know, do I? I'm looking out for yer.

Pause.

PETA. Thanks.

MARION. Don't need to say thanks neither. (*Pause.*) I mean . . . you know, say what you like. I just didn't want you to feel

like you had anything to thank me for. Do it for anyone.
Just looking out. People don't do that much, it's a bloody
shame. I think everyone has a . . . responsibility. It isn't just
about you and yours, you know what I mean?

Silence.

PETA. How late is it?

MARION. How early more like. Half past five.

PETA. Next day again.

MARION. Is there someone I can ring?

PETA. What for?

MARION. For you?

PETA. No. I'm alright.

MARION. I can sit with you. Long as you like. I don't mind.

PETA. Ta.

MARION. If you don't mind –

PETA. No. Thanks.

Pause.

MARION. Are you in trouble?

PETA. What sort of trouble?

MARION. I don't know. I'm asking, aren't I? I wouldn't know
. . . comes in all sorts of ways, doesn't it? Trouble. My
trouble mightn't be yours and . . . vice-versa. You are
pregnant, aren't you?

PETA. No.

MARION. It's nothing to do with me. I'm not going to tell
anyone. (*Beat.*) You are over sixteen though?

PETA. Yeah.

Silence.

MARION. Mother's intuition. And these . . . (*She holds up the
bits of paper and pamphlet* PETA *took from under the bed*

before.) I wasn't snooping. They were out, lying all over the bed.

Pause.

What you doing here anyway?

PETA. I'm staying here.

MARION. Since when?

PETA. I just moved in for a bit.

MARION. What happened to the other girl? The student?

PETA. She's away . . . gone home for the holidays.

MARION. Funny one, her. She your mate?

PETA. No.

MARION. What you doing here then?

PETA. She's me mate's cousin . . . she's letting me stay. For a bit.

MARION. Sort your head out?

PETA. Yeah.

MARION. All on your own.

PETA. I'm best on me own. Always forget that.

MARION. Lonely that though, eh?

PETA. I only get lonely if I'm with the wrong people.

MARION. Who's the wrong person then?

PETA. No one. The place . . . just wore me down. I'm only young . . . Felt old there. Felt like everything was set out. Set in stone, like you couldn't change. London's big –

MARION. Too big.

PETA. You can be who you like.

Pause.

MARION. You shouldn't be drinking. Not in your condition. Not like that.

Pause.

Are you with him?

PETA. Who?

MARION. Whoever's responsible for –

PETA. No . . . One night. Don't know him.

MARION (*gesturing towards the photo*). Who's that then?

Pause.

PETA. Me dad.

MARION. Will he be worried about you?

PETA. I haven't seen him since I was seven. He left.

MARION. Right. You still put his picture up?

PETA. He's still me dad.

MARION. You're not in any state to be on your own. You need looking after –

PETA. I don't –

MARION. I can only do so much.

PETA. I don't want any help. I'm alright. I'll be alright. Thank you . . . for this.

MARION. I told you I don't want any. Haven't even done anything. Do it for anyone. I'm just thinking, if you've got people worrying about you . . . it's a living hell. I don't sleep any more . . . it drives you mad. Literally, makes you . . . mad. Waiting.

PETA. What you waiting for?

Pause.

MARION. That's a bloody good question, Peta. I'm not completely sure.

Silence.

My daughter's a bit older than you. Couple of years. She lives . . . lived with me. I wait for her. She's always back

after a few weeks but it doesn't make you feel better in
between. Toughest job in the world, being a parent. You'll
know about that soon enough.

Silence.

Well, you will.

PETA. Where is she?

MARION. I don't know.

PETA. She's missing?

MARION. She comes and goes. She got . . . caught up in stuff.
Think I must have been blind. Looking back. It just ran up
at me. Hardly any warning. She turned into a pencil
drawing of herself. Dead eyes. She'll be back when she
needs money.

Silence.

(*Gesturing to photograph.*) You can tell a lot from
photographs. My friend reads them . . . like fortune-telling.
Looks at people's faces, tells you what's going to happen. I
didn't believe it 'til she did mine and all this stuff came
true. We could get a taxi to the hospital. Get you looked at.

PETA. What for?

MARION. See if you're OK. We should –

PETA. I don't want to –

MARION. It's silly not to get you looked at.

PETA. I don't want to.

MARION. I feel a responsibility. To do what's right.

PETA. I'm OK.

MARION. You're in a mess.

PETA. I feel a bit better.

MARION. That was some topple.

PETA. Sounded worse than it was.

MARION. You shouldn't be drinking.

PETA. I shouldn't be lots of things.

Pause.

MARION. It's frightening . . . bringing up a kid. Being alone.

PETA. I don't want it.

MARION. You're scared. It's normal. You need your family around you . . . your mum.

PETA. She threw me out. (*Pause.*) I left. Bit of both.

MARION. Mothers and daughters. She'll come round. She's worrying about you, s'all. Trying to do that 'tough love' thing.

PETA. It was four years ago.

MARION. I see.

Silence.

It's a difficult time.

PETA. Are you religious?

MARION. Why?

PETA. You sound like a vicar.

MARION. I'm concerned about you . . . that's all. Religion or not. Concern. Young girl on her own . . . I've been in your shoes, Peta.

PETA. No, you haven't. No one's ever been in my shoes. No one's ever been in anyone else's shoes but their own. It's just something people say.

Pause.

MARION. Are you sure you weren't trying to do something daft?

PETA. Depends what you mean by daft.

MARION. You know what I mean, Peta.

PETA. I wasn't –

MARION. You can say if you were. I understand that . . . hopelessness.

PETA. I'm not hopeless. I've got loads of hope.

MARION. Good.

PETA. I'm a glass half-full sort of person.

MARION. I'm sure you are. But . . . you're not in the best of places at the moment, are yer? Inside . . . In your head? That's alright to say . . . doesn't mean you're not –

PETA. What's your daughter called?

MARION. Beatrice.

Silence.

Beatrice Elizabeth Ann McBride. Beatrice after my mother, Elizabeth and Ann just because I liked them. Her intials are BEAM. Like Sunbeam . . . I liked that. I didn't notice until we went for her birth certificate.

PETA. Did you throw her out?

MARION. No.

Pause.

Threatened it. Said never again and meant it with all my heart. I meant it every single time. (*Pause.*) Sick of the sound of me own voice. Like a broken record. I said, 'You've broken my heart,' then I'd beg her not to go. She'd say, 'Make your mind up.' She thinks she's funny. She was I suppose . . . is . . . I don't know. Anyway, I never tell her to go any more. Just give her money and say I'll give her a bit more if she hangs on a couple of days longer. It confuses me . . . I get very confused and I try to tell her that n'all but . . . every time I say anything about the way I feel, she comes back with 'You think *you're* confused' or heartbroken or disgusted . . . whatever it was . . . 'How d'yer think I feel?' and I beg her to tell me . . . like it's a little opening, a little chink of light . . . but she never does. (*Pause.*) Didn't think I'd done such a terrible job but then how do you explain it? I'd rather blame myself anyway, gives me something constructive to do with all that . . . hurting. She said that to me anyway . . . blamed me . . . she said, 'You've let me down so badly.' I should have been tougher apparently . . . given her some backbone. Made her strong . . . not given in to her all the time. (*Pause.*) I feel like I've . . . stopped sometimes. Actually just stopped. That's not the worst of it by far. Stopping. S'quite . . . nice. In a funny way. A change.

PETA. I'm sorry for yer.

MARION. Don't . . . thank you. Everyone's got their – Do you miss your mum?

Pause.

PETA. No.

MARION. Do you ever . . . do you see her, speak to her?

PETA. I phone sometimes. Home. Every now and again. It rings out mostly. She's hardly ever there. I don't say anything.

MARION. Why not?

PETA. I just want to check she hasn't moved.

Pause.

MARION. Beatrice rings me sometimes. She never says anything. I just sit with her for a bit. On the phone. I used to try to get her to talk to me. Now I just sit with her . . . listening to her breathe. It's like she's a baby again. I feel close to her. I like to think she does it for me. (*Pause.*) What would make you feel better?

PETA. Dunno.

MARION. Why don't you have a nice bath?

PETA. I feel like I might go mad sometimes.

MARION. That means you won't. I wouldn't worry, only sane people feel like they're mad. Until they are, then they can't tell. Have a nice warm bath.

PETA. S'like I can't breathe.

MARION. I could run it for you.

PETA. It's OK.

MARION. First thing I do when Beatrice shows up. She sits in it for hours. Makes me feel like I'm . . . doing something. Like a mother. I wash her back. Afterwards, I dry her hair for her. Comb it through, like when she was little.

PETA. I don't want one.

MARION. I dread to think how often she gets to have a bath when she's not at home. She smells. That's heartbreaking . . . having your daughter smell like that. I can't believe I'm saying that out loud. That makes me just –

PETA. I don't smell.

MARION. I never said you do. What makes you think you smell?

Pause.

PETA. I had one this morning.

MARION. It'll help you sleep. Have you got any lavender oil?

PETA. No.

MARION. Would you like some?

PETA. What for?

MARION. Your bath. Put a bit in . . . stick it under the tap. Helps you relax. I've got some.

PETA. Alright.

MARION. Shall I get it?

PETA. OK.

MARION. Will you be alright? You look a bit . . . pale.

PETA. I've got pale skin.

MARION. More pale. Paler . . . than you were before. (*Pause.*) I won't be a minute then.

MARION *exits, leaving the door ajar. PETA sits at the edge of the bed, feet on the floor, hands in her lap. MARION returns, carrying a towel and a bottle of lavender oil. She goes into the bathroom and turns the bath taps on.*

(*From the bathroom.*) You only need a bit. (*Pause.*) It's concentrated.

Silence.

Coming in from the bathroom, MARION *sits beside* PETA *on the bed.*

I brought a towel. Good job, the one in there's screwed up on the floor. Sopping wet.

PETA. You can go back to bed.

MARION. I'll stay until you've had your bath.

PETA. I won't try and drown myself.

MARION. I should hope not. I meant . . . fainting. Slipping and banging your head or something.

PETA. You're a mum, aren't yer?

MARION. I wish. Seems a bit . . . late for that now. No, God forgive me for that. Jesus. I am a mother.

PETA. You've been here ages.

MARION. I don't mind. If you're feeling a bit . . . down.

PETA. I'm OK.

MARION. Would you like to be on your own?

PETA. I think so . . . I don't know.

MARION. It's just, I'll worry, you see, imagine how I'd feel if – I won't sleep anyway.

PETA. You could –

MARION. I could sit. While you have a bath. Out here. You could talk if you wanted. Leave the door ajar.

Pause. PETA *goes into the bathroom, turns the taps off. She is getting into the bath as* MARION *lights another cigarette and sits on the floor outside the bathroom, her back against the wall.*

Is it too hot? You shouldn't have it too hot when you're – Put a bit of cold in, if it is.

Pause.

You have people back. Sometimes.

Silence.

I'm not saying anything by that.

Pause.

I don't sleep and I can hear . . . not words, just conversations. Voices. Not what you're talking about. I don't listen.

Silence.

I wasn't getting at anything.

Pause.

People come and go. It isn't any of my business. I wasn't –

PETA. I don't like the dark.

MARION. Right.

Silence.

Do you smoke, Peta?

PETA. No.

MARION. That's something. I smoked. With Beatrice. There wasn't much about it then. No one really said. I wouldn't now . . . if it was now. Good for you.

PETA. I've never smoked.

MARION. No?

PETA. I tried. It made me sick.

MARION. Good. Disgusting habit. I don't need to worry any more. Just me.

Pause.

Are you alright in there?

PETA. Yeah.

MARION. Do you want anything?

PETA. No. Thanks.

Silence.

MARION. It's hard, Peta . . . being on your own.

Silence.

I was on my own. With Beatrice, well, after she was about two or so. That's what I wanted, mind. Her dad wasn't all that bad, just . . . neither use nor ornament really. Just something I fell into. Sounds terrible, that, doesn't it? He wasn't bad really . . . did his bit even though he had a chip on his shoulder size of a fucking small planet. Can't quite remember the point when that tailed off . . . him being good, not the chip on his shoulder. There weren't any great ructions, no big fights. It was all quite quiet really, he just tiptoed out gradually. I felt quite sorry for him. He said he didn't have a place.

PETA *enters from the bathroom. A towel around her, her hair dripping wet.*

PETA. People come and go.

MARION. You're dripping your hair everywhere.

MARION *goes into the bathroom and gets a hand towel.* PETA *sits on the bed and* MARION *starts to dry her hair for her.*

Sometimes now though, I think . . . if he'd been around, you know . . . not so much that I think things would have been any different, but I would have been able to share it. You know. (*Pause.*) There you go.

PETA. Thank you.

MARION. Feel a bit better?

PETA. Yeah.

MARION. Lavender oil. Why don't you get back in them pyjamas? Get yourself into bed.

As she speaks, MARION *fetches the pyjamas from the bathroom and hands them to* PETA.

I won't look. Seen it all before anyway.

PETA *takes them but goes back into the bathroom to get changed. She comes back out and climbs into bed.* MARION *fusses around, tucking the covers in, before sitting on the chair.*

I'll just sit here 'til you're off again. I won't sleep anyway so I may as well not sleep up here, eh? I'll just wait . . . until you're off.

PETA *settles down to sleep. Silence for a few seconds before* MARION *begins to hum the same song as before.*

Blackout.

Scene Five

PETA *sits on the floor. The bed has been put back into a sofa and she is leaning against it. The sports bag with her things in, by her side. There is a knock at the door. She stands up and opens it.* COLIN *stands, out of view.* PETA *stands in the doorway, silent, timid – she acts quite childlike in his presence.*

COLIN. Hello.

Pause.

PETA. Hello.

Long pause. They look at each other.

COLIN. Can I come in or what? Feel like a bouncer leant against here –

PETA. Yeah.

COLIN. Pools-man or something.

She turns and walks into the flat. COLIN follows her. She sits on the sofa with her back to him. He stands. They are silent for ages.

Crap in 'ere, innit?

Silence.

Like a fuckin' squat or something. Stinks.

Pause.

PETA. Do you want – Can I get you something? Tea or something? Are you hungry?

COLIN *shakes his head.*

Got milk?

Silence.

I can put the heater on. I'm shivering.

COLIN. It's warm.

PETA. I'm shivering.

COLIN. Put it on then.

PETA. I'm not bothered.

COLIN. Not bothered?

PETA. No. I can put a jumper on.

Pause.

COLIN. Go on then.

PETA. I'm not that –

COLIN. Put a jumper on. You're shivering.

PETA *goes to the bathroom door and fetches CHANTELLE's cardigan from the chest of drawers. She sits down again, huddled. Silence for a few moments, COLIN watches her.*

That's nice.

PETA. Thanks.

COLIN. Is it new?

PETA. Sort of.

COLIN. It's nice.

PETA. Thanks.

COLIN. Not your sort of thing.

> PETA *wraps her arms around herself.*

> You're still cold?

PETA. I'm alright.

> *Silence.*

> Sit down.

> *Pause.*

COLIN. I'm OK.

> *Pause.*

> I thought you'd grown out of this.

> *Silence.*

> Yer listening, Peta?

PETA. Yeah.

COLIN. I thought you'd –

PETA. Yeah.

COLIN. Grown out of this –

PETA. Yeah.

COLIN. Yeah what?

> *Pause.*

> Yes. What?

PETA. Did you read me letter?

COLIN. I thought all this . . . fuckin' arsing around, thought it was finished with.

PETA. I signed it 'love'. I spelt it 'l-o-v-e' not 'l-u-v', like you don't mean it.

COLIN. Thought we could . . . move on. Especially now –

PETA. Yeah.

COLIN. Yeah what?

PETA. Yeah . . . we can . . . still can.

He walks over to the photo. Picks it up, studies it. Holds it.

COLIN. Thought things were gonna be different.

PETA. Did you read my letter?

He puts the photo back.

COLIN. No.

PETA. Why not?

COLIN. I didn't need to, I knew what it'd say. Propped up on the table like that.

Silence.

Doesn't need opening, does it? Says it all with . . . yer name on it. Fuckin' . . . Dear fuckin' John.

PETA. It wasn't like that.

Pause.

COLIN. You promised. Yer not a kid no more, Peta. You can't say shit and not mean it. You said it was –

PETA. It is. It's finished with. I want to come home.

He sits. PETA *still has her back towards him.*

COLIN. Turn round.

PETA *turns.*

I took holiday . . . well, unpaid leave. They don't normally allow that . . . it doesn't happen if you're not permanent.

But I had a word with the site manager. Told him, like.
Explained it all and he said it was . . . what was it . . .
extenuating, I think that was the word, extenuating
circumstances. Do you know what that is? I didn't 'til the
other day. Someone told me. Do you know?

PETA. Yeah.

COLIN. That's what he told me anyway. (*Pause.*) I always
thought he was a prick . . . have I mentioned him? Stuart?
Say he was a prick?

PETA. Yeah.

COLIN. Well yeah . . . I always thought so. He's alright as it
goes. Married like . . . got a family. Two little boys. Makes
a difference that, I reckon . . . people understand more when
they've got a family . . . it makes you more . . . well, you
know, you put yourself, don't yer . . . in other people's
shoes. He said he'd tell everyone I were ill . . . there's
something going round so it makes it – it doesn't look
weird, you know . . . I didn't want him saying, didn't want
everyone knowing. Worse than women, them lot.

Pause.

PETA. Why didn't you come yesterday when I phoned? I've
been waiting –

COLIN. Have yer?

PETA. Been sat here ready.

COLIN. I did. Come last night. Bombed it. Got here by half
seven. (*Beat.*) I sat in the car. Just wanted to – Got meself in
knots. Felt like I was . . . I got scared of meself. You know
when you think you just might fuckin' – Needed a bit of
time to just . . . get me head into gear. Found this little B&B
in King's Cross . . . it was alright . . . well, it was a fucking
shithole actually. Minty as fuck. I slept on top of the covers
or lay on top of the covers. I didn't sleep. (*Pause.*) Prozzies
striding up and down, right outside the window. Getting
picked up by these dirty-lookin' fuckers. Old men. Fucking
depressing that. Fucking worrying. Sitting there . . .
thinking all sorts.

Silence.

I was scared to come . . . in a way. Wanted to come more than anything, but I was just so fucking scared of what . . .

Silence.

Can you imagine, Peta? Eh, what that's like? (*Pause.*) No, fuckin' seriously . . . I'm asking you. Do you have any idea what that's like?

PETA. No.

COLIN. No?

PETA. I just –

COLIN. It's fuckin' shit.

Silence.

You've got no idea because I wouldn't do that to you, would I? That's why you've got no idea. Cos I wouldn't do that to you, Peta. I wouldn't fucking do that to you.

PETA. I didn't get your messages.

COLIN. I didn't leave any. Why the fuck should I leave you any messages?

PETA. To find out where I was.

COLIN. I wanted you to miss me.

PETA. I tried you sometimes. Your phone was off. You left it off. You didn't read me letter.

COLIN. Wrecks your head. I wanted you to miss me.

PETA. I did.

Pause.

I couldn't ever sleep. I thought you might be awake too. Wondering.

COLIN. They're all the same, those rooms, aren't they? Wherever you go, it's that fucking standard-issue horrible shitty-brown wallpaper . . . fuckin' . . . hospital blankets. You can go anywhere, North or South . . . get in one of them places. Same set-up. (*Beat.*) And who stays there? Who stays in those places, eh? Cos you don't choose to, surely. You don't wanna be there. You end up there. Like some fucking twilight zone. Like some fucking halfway house.

Silence.

I went looking for yer. I did look for yer.

PETA. I tried to leave a message but I didn't . . . I couldn't think what to say.

COLIN. You need to do something. Feel helpless if you're just sat there . . . like you're letting shit happen. Bad things. I even tried your mother's. Fucking last resort. Fucking loved that, didn't she? Loved the fact you'd left. Doesn't care where yer are, just fucking loved it that you'd left me. Still calling me a fucking cradle-snatcher. She's got a fucking short memory, your mother. If you can call her that.

PETA. Don't, Col.

COLIN. She kept saying, 'My daughter.' I said, 'You haven't got a daughter, Irene, you said that yourself, four years ago.' (*Pause.*) She should be fucking grateful. If I hadn't come along –

PETA. I couldn't find any words. There's loads . . . in me head.

Pause.

Can yer . . . listen to me? Please Col. Can yer listen to me?

COLIN. I'm listening to you.

PETA. I miss you.

COLIN. I'm here.

PETA. I have done . . . missed you.

COLIN. Have you? Only it wouldn't . . . it doesn't seem like that . . . does that make sense? I'm not going mad here, am I?

PETA. No. I know –

COLIN. I'm not imagining shit here, am I?

PETA. Can you . . . can you be – Not. Can you talk . . . I just wanted something.

COLIN. You don't make any sense to me, Peta.

COLIN stands and starts to pace slowly around the room. He stops and picks up the photo.

I'm not very . . .

Pause.

PETA. What?

COLIN. Photo . . . genic. Am I?

Pause.

It means I don't look good in photos.

PETA. I know.

COLIN. Then why didn't you answer me?

PETA. Cos it wasn't a question.

COLIN. It was.

Pause.

It was sort of anyway. It was a sort of question. I suppose I was asking – it was like fishing –

PETA. I don't know what you mean –

COLIN. For a compliment. It was like I wanted to you to say 'You do, Col . . . you look nice in photeys. You look like someone I love. It's your face.'

PETA. It is your face.

COLIN. Do you love it?

PETA. The photey?

COLIN. My face.

Pause.

PETA. Yeah.

COLIN. You've got it up. That's something, eh? You must want to see my face.

PETA. I do.

COLIN. Bullshit.

Pause.

PETA. I wanted to see what it was like to leave home. For a bit.

COLIN. You left home four years ago. You haven't been back since. Y'not satisfied with that?

PETA. That wasn't me home.

He puts the photo back on the chest and sits down. They look at each other.

You are.

COLIN. But you wanted to leave –

PETA. I wanted to see –

COLIN. I saw your dad the other week. Coming out The Lion . . . didn't recognise me. I had to go up . . . proper stand in his face, like . . . he starts leaning on me . . . fucking hate the way he does that, don't you? He knows he knows me but he just can't think where from and I go, 'Alright Gerry, mate, it's Colin.' Blank. I'm like, 'I go with your daughter,' and he goes, 'Which one?' and I say, 'Peta, mate . . . you've only got one. Remember her?' It has been a while though, eh? He give me fifty pee for yer.

Silence.

PETA. I got scared.

COLIN. What of?

PETA. Not being . . . being without you. It was . . . I just wanted to see –

COLIN. See what?

PETA. Stuff. Just for a bit, Col. Just for a bit. It was because of when we came. That day. At the very beginning. I wanted to go back to the aquarium.

COLIN. You never said much. I thought you thought it was crap.

PETA. I loved it.

COLIN. I felt stupid. Thought you'd think it was for kids.

PETA. I was a kid –

COLIN. Old enough . . . Don't – You know what I meant . . . Thought I should have taken yer somewhere . . . fancy . . . to a big show or –

PETA. It was me favourite day. (*Pause.*) I just wanted to see.

Pause.

COLIN. What did you see, then?

PETA. Nothing really.

COLIN. Nothing?

PETA. Not really.

Pause.

COLIN. I painted the little room. Morning light. It's yellow really. Pale yellow. I bought a . . . thing strip to go round the top . . . a border. It's got rocking horses on it.

Pause.

I just went ahead. Sorry.

PETA. It's alright.

COLIN. Yellow's either, isn't it?

PETA. Yeah.

Pause.

COLIN. I liked doing it. It was good for me head. Bit weird without you, but good. Therapeutic.

Pause.

Is it too late . . . am I too late?

PETA. No.

COLIN. But what did you come for? You were *intending* to . . . you come here with intent.

PETA. For a bit.

COLIN. Two weeks.

PETA. No longer than that.

COLIN. Two weeks. Fourteen nights. Inside my fuckin' head.

Pause.

PETA. Will you talk to me . . . don't get angry about it all, I didn't . . . I feel sick.

COLIN. Be sick.

PETA. I can't . . . I just feel it –

COLIN. Put your fingers down your throat.

PETA. I can't.

COLIN. You'll have to take a bag –

PETA. I think I –

COLIN. You'll have to take a bag in the car . . . because you're not going to puke shite all over the car seats . . . I've just had it cleaned.

PETA. Yes.

COLIN. You'll need to get your shit together. Your stuff.

PETA. I've got it. I've got it ready.

COLIN. I don't know what you're trying to do to me . . . I fuckin' –

PETA. I was always coming back. I got me stuff ready. I didn't bring much.

COLIN. I saw Rachel. I went to see her. Explain you weren't feeling too bright. She was a bit shitty but I told her about the baby and she was alright. (*Pause.*) She said you can go back, no problem, like.

PETA. Colin. I don't want to go back there. I hate –

COLIN. You can go in on Monday. She won't be weird with yer.

PETA. I don't want to work there any more.

COLIN. She said she can put you on the phones. Take yer out the warehouse. No more lifting shit. It's all cleared. Get back to normal.

Pause.

Get back to normal.

PETA. This is why I wanted yer to read the letter –

COLIN. All I've done . . . All I want to do . . . just look after you . . . just take care. Of you. Have I not done that?

PETA. You're my family. I wrote it all down.

COLIN. I'm your boyfriend.

PETA. You're more.

He moves toward her and she flinches slightly.

Col . . . please don't –

COLIN. What you on about?

PETA. I'm –

Pause. They stand looking at each other. COLIN *moves slowly towards her and takes hold of her face.*

COLIN. I don't know why you do stuff like this . . . what I do . . . for you. Everything. Is that fair . . . do you think?

PETA. I feel . . . broken. I wish I didn't have to explain –

He puts his arms around her. Stiffly, she moves hers from by her sides to around his waist.

COLIN. I feel broken. I am broken. I'm broken in the middle of the night. I'm broken going to the shops. I'm broken watching the telly . . . just waiting for the day when I'm not . . . broken. That's you doing that. I wasn't like that before.

PETA. Please don't, Colin –

COLIN. Please don't what, Colin? Please don't fucking what? Please don't breathe, Colin. Please don't put a roof over me head. Please don't take me in and save me from shit. Please come and get me please. Please don't leave me please, get the fuck out. Please fucking don't. Please fucking don't what?

PETA. It was just for a bit. I wanted to do some things. It doesn't matter now. I want to share it all with yer. Can we go?

COLIN. I don't wanna have to keep looking over me shoulder.

PETA. Col . . . will you forget it? Forget about it. Can we go home?

COLIN. What's the rush . . . You got someone coming round?

PETA. No.

COLIN. What's that?

PETA (*chewing her nails*). No.

COLIN. You're making me nervous.

She chews her nails.

Will you stop doing that fuckin' thing? Like a kid . . . fuckin' baby or something.

PETA. I can't help it.

COLIN. You're getting worse. I need it the other way. I need a bit back. D'yer hear me?

PETA. Yeah.

COLIN. I need a bit back. Five years down the line. I need a bit of something. Did it all for you then. Somewhere to stay that wasn't . . . that was safe. Somewhere safe. A home. Need a bit . . . back.

PETA. It was just for a bit –

COLIN. Get back to normal.

PETA. I didn't like it being alone. I had the fear.

COLIN. You're telling me about the fear? Get your fucking things together.

PETA. Battle-fear. I'm scared of what I know. I've got me bag. I've got all me things.

COLIN. I'll get the car.

PETA. I read the other day that battle-fear, Col . . . battle-fear and lovesickness are the same thing. I knew exactly what that was about.

COLIN. You wanna watch that . . . thinking you're a cut above. Talking shit.

PETA. I just thought – if you'd listen . . . it could be alright – I want to tell you things.

Silence. COLIN *leans against the chest, arms folded.*

COLIN. Tell me fucking things.

PETA. Little things.

COLIN. Two minutes.

PETA. When I first got here I spent a day . . . a whole day on buses. I got a Travelcard and I just got on different buses. Like we did that day. I just thought I'd see where I ended up. But it wasn't like when we did it.

COLIN. I'll get the car.

PETA. I haven't finished. You said you'd listen –

COLIN. You got on buses –

PETA. I went to Crystal Palace first. I thought . . . I imagined something different. Crystal Palace. I bought a fried egg sandwich from this café . . . by the terminus. And it had shell in it. I wanted to cry. That made me want to cry. I felt about eight . . . or something. I wanted you. (*Beat.*) Then I got back on a bus and I went to Victoria and I got another bus. A 38. I just sat on it 'til I had to get off. And I got off and just walked for a bit . . . just walking. I turned down this road . . . this little road. It was just normal. Just houses, cars . . . but at the end of it was this sort of . . . it

was like this Roman building like . . . huge columns . . .
colonnades . . . a pointed roof bit. Really gorgeous and a
bit, you know . . . mad . . . because it was just there at the
top of this road with houses and cars and that wasn't the
part though. Along the top of it . . . the whole width of it
was – it wasn't switched on but there were neon tubes.
Lettering that said, 'Everything's going to be alright.' Just
that. Everything's going to be alright.

Silence.

I went back yesterday – before I phoned yer . . . and it was
just rubble. Thought I'd imagined it. Asked this woman
cleaning the windows of her house. I asked her if it had said
that and she said, 'Yeah'. I would have liked to show it to
you but it isn't there any more. That's it.

Pause. COLIN *stands by the door, looking at her.*

I've got me stuff ready.

COLIN. I'll bring it round. Five minutes, yeah?

COLIN *leaves.* PETA *takes the photo and, wrapping a
T-shirt around it first, places it carefully into the bag. She
goes into the kitchen and gets herself a glass of milk. She
comes back into the living area and sits on the sofa, holding
the bag in one hand and drinking her milk with the other.*

End.

A Nick Hern Book

How Love Is Spelt first published in Great Britain
as a paperback original in 2004 by Nick Hern Books Limited,
14 Larden Road, London W3 7ST in association with
The Bush Theatre, London

Cover image: Getty Images / Stem Design

Typeset by Country Setting, Kingsdown, Kent CT14 8ES

Printed and bound in Great Britain by Cox and Wyman Ltd,
Reading, Berks

A CIP catalogue record for this book is available from
the British Library

ISBN 1 85459 849 X